— In Search of —

OLD BILL

The Life of
Thomas Rafferty

⸻❦⸻

The Inspiration
for Bairnsfather's
Greatest Creation

"It could be worse: you could be in the same 'ole as Belcher!"

A cartoon by Rob Houghton, a wonderfully talented poet of working class
Birmingham. It is based on Bairnsfather's cartoon of 'Old Bill'
and highlights the similarity to Thomas Rafferty.

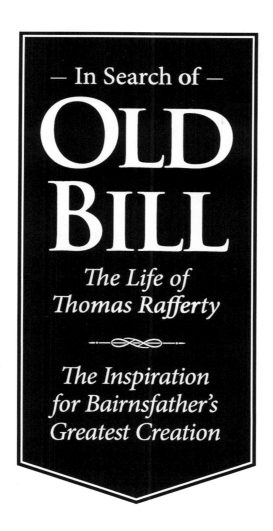

— In Search of —

OLD BILL

The Life of
Thomas Rafferty

The Inspiration
for Bairnsfather's
Greatest Creation

JOHN BELCHER

Edited by Thomas Small
Foreword by Carl Chinn

BREWIN BOOKS

BREWIN BOOKS
19 Enfield Ind. Estate,
Redditch,
Worcestershire,
B97 6BY
www.brewinbooks.com

Published by Brewin Books 2022

A CIP catalogue record for this book is available from the British Library.

ISBN: 978-1-85858-747-9

Printed and bound in Great Britain
by 4edge Ltd.

IN REMEMBRANCE OF THE FORGOTTEN
HEROES OF THE GREAT WAR

"They shall grow not old, as we that are left grow old,
Age shall not weary them nor the years condemn,
At the going down of the sun and in the morning
We shall remember them."

Laurence Binyon

In Memory of my father
Frank Roland Belcher 1/7th Batt R.W.R., WWII.

Contents

Part III: In Memoriam

Acknowledgements

This book is the culmination of many years research which I have finally sought to document for the sake of posterity, and the memory of Thomas Rafferty himself. I could not have produced it without the input of the following people that have aided and contributed to this research.

I am grateful to Thomas Small for his work in editing my original manuscript. He was able to provide a convincing and engaging narrative based upon my original research.

Some of my research regarding the Rafferty papers was published in 1992 after contacting the Holts, the biographer's of Bruce Bairnsfather. My research has also been the basis for several articles published in national and local newspapers and journals. Naming Thomas Rafferty as 'Old Bill', *The Independent* published the article "Old Bill identified after 77 years in that 'Ole", May 1992. Later *The Sunday Times* also published the article, "Old on, That's Uncle Tom in that 'Ole", (November 2015) that discusses my recent discovery of the Bairnsfather article in the context of my research. Other published articles included *The Stand To: the journal of the Western Front Association*, (1992), *Bygone Birmingham*, (issues 6, 7, 24), and *The Antelope: the bulletin of the Fusiliers Association*, (1992).

Some of my original research was published in two books on the Great War: the 2001 edition of *In Search of The Better 'Ole* by Toni and Valmi Holt (pp. 240-241), and the book *Meet at Dawn Unarmed: the diaries of Captain Robert Hamilton* (the 2009 edition by Andrew Hamilton and Alan Reed, pp. 35, 99, 195).

I contacted the Lord Mayor of Birmingham, Sir Richard Knowles in 1995, and presented him with the information I had at the time. He was proud to find out 'Old Bill' was a Brummie, remembering him as a hero of his younger days. He sent my information to Birmingham Reference Library to be catalogued and housed in the Birmingham Collection Archives.

Mrs Ivy Dobbins, the daughter of Thomas and Kate Rafferty.

Mrs Edna Olive Belcher, Ivy Rafferty's cousin.

Lynne Taylor, T H Rafferty's great niece.

Mr C B Rollins, Royal Warwickshire Regiment. As the son of Private S Rollins, who was a friend of Thomas Rafferty's, Cyril would provide a valuable link to the original 'Old Bill'.

Janet Montgomery who helped compile the website www.thomasrafferty.org.uk (now superseded by this book), which helped to raise the profile of Thomas Rafferty.

I once lived next to a Bill Philpotts who showed me a 'swagger stick' with a Warwick's silver knob that had belonged to his relative, a sergeant in the R.W.R. During the ensuing conversation I was to find out that his relative had played football against a Saxon regiment during the Christmas truce.

Professor Carl Chinn CSA MBE for his encouragement in continuing my research.

Robert Betteridge, Social Historian, who provided information on Birmingham's memorials.

Southerden S B, a researcher at The Royal Green Jackets Museum, confirmed that John Rafferty, Thomas's older brother, served with the King's Royal Rifles during the First World War, which later became part of the 'Green Jackets'.

Paul Reed, Military Historian. Paul provided information on the history of the First World War based on official documents relating to military operations in France and Belgium during 1915, originally compiled by Brigadier General J E Edmonds, Captain G C Wynne and Major E Becke.

Dr Bob Bushaway, Military Historian.

J Evans (5114819 Royal Warwickshire Regiment).

Gemma Byrne and Rowena Rowlands for their research.

D S Taylor BA (Hons) Transport Historian.

Bill Harriman of the *Antiques Road Show* for acknowledging the importance of the archive of documents once held by Kate Rafferty.

Howard Williamson for his helpful guidance, providing me with information regarding Commemorative Peace medals.

Saty Madhav, for the professional restoration of original photographs from Kate Rafferty's archive.

The Elders of The Church of The Seventh Day, Birmingham.

Foreword

In March, 1918, just a few months before the end of the First World War, a group of journalists from British, American and Dominion newspapers visited Birmingham, the metropolis of the United Kingdom's munitions industry. Spending a week there, they visited various works and were staggered at the colossal scale of Birmingham's war-time production. People worked 'night and day, without talk, with sleeves rolled up, and your shoulder to the task'. So vast were the operations that 'this industrial epic will never be written, for the simple reason that no man is equal to the task. There is an article in every workshop, a volume in every trade'. In each and every hive of industry, work proceeded 'to the roar of the furnace, the hiss of escaping steam, the rhythmic throb of the engine, the crash of hydraulic presses, the metallic ring of stamping machines, and the clatter of lighter operations at the benches'. The minds of the journalists were left with nothing but confused impressions. But out of this welter of ideas, imperfectly grasped and imperfectly correlated, emerged two very distinct conceptions: one of the immensity of effort and output and the other of the power of organisation.

With a change more startling than that ever produced by the turn of a kaleidoscope, Birmingham's industries had converted totally to the needs of a total war. Jewellers made anti-gas apparatus; firms noted for artistic work manufactured an intricate type of hand grenade; cycle-makers devoted themselves to fuses and shells; world-famous pen-makers adapted machinery to produce cartridge clips; railway carriage companies turned out artillery wagons, tanks and aeroplanes; and chemical works attended to deadly T.N.T. Other factories made shells, fuses, and rifles by the million, Lewis guns by the thousand, and artillery limbers by the hundreds – as well as monster aeroplanes, battalions of tanks, aeroplane engines, and big guns. In fact, Birmingham had so transformed itself for the purpose of war, that 'it is well that the world should be made aware of the magnitude and the thoroughness of the achievement'.

That remarkable transformation of moving swiftly from civilian output to the needs of the war effort was acknowledged by King George V in a visit on 22nd and 23rd July, 1915. Nominally secret, it quickly gained attention after his arrival. After first speaking to wounded servicemen at the First Southern General Hospital at Birmingham University, he spent the afternoon at the

King's Norton Metal Company. The next day, he went first to the Kynoch works at Witton. At its peak it would employ 18,000 people, and it had guaranteed each week to produce 25 million rifle cartridges, 300,000 revolver cartridges, 500,000 cartridge clips, 110,000 18-pounder brass cases, and 300 tons of cordite. These figures were impressive, all the more so as it took 102 operations to manufacture a single rifle cartridge whilst the limit of accuracy prescribed in nearly all the finished dimensions was within one-thousandth of an inch. Bar for the cordite, everything involved in the production was manufactured in Birmingham.

Thence, the King was taken to the Birmingham Small Arms works at Small Heath, where the increase in output of rifles was astonishing. From an average of 135 rifles made per week in the five years before the war, production had increased to about 10,000, and for Lewis guns it had risen from 50 a week to 2,000. Additionally, the BSA manufactured bicycles and motor bicycles for the Army, and 150,000 aeroplane parts per week. From there, the King went to the Metropolitan Carriage Wagon works at Saltley. Part of the Vickers-Metropolitan group of factories in Birmingham it also made a considerable contribution to the war effort. Tanks, aeroplanes and 'other of the larger engines of war' were manufactured at the wagon works; whilst 38 million fuses and large numbers of anti-aircraft shells and naval and field cases were produced at the Electric and Ordnance Accessories factories in Aston and Ward End. Finally, after a tour of the Birmingham Metal and Munitions Company at Adderley Park, the royal visit ended at the nearby works of Wolseley Motors, which would build over 4,000 cars for the military and 4,500 aero engines. The King was encouraged by what he saw. In particular, he praised both the successful manner in which factories had been diverted from their customary civil occupations and how 'unfamiliar labour, including that of many women and girls who previously had never seen the inside of a factory, had been brought in and trained to new occupations'. Indeed, he was astonished at how quickly this inexperienced labour had adapted itself to unfamiliar tasks and how keen the women were to obtain the largest possible output

Three years after the war ended, in 1921, the Prime Minister, Mr. Lloyd George emphasised the importance of Birmingham's contribution to the war in a speech at the Town Hall. He declared that 'the country, the empire and the world owe to the skill, the ingenuity, the industry and the resource of Birmingham a deep debt of gratitude, and as an old Minister of Munitions, and as the present Prime Minister, I am here to thank you from the bottom of my heart for the services which you rendered at that perilous moment.'

Those were not the only services rendered by Birmingham's citizens as 150,000 men answered the call to arms. Of these, 12,320 died and 35,000 came home disabled. Many more must have suffered post-traumatic stress. Although these Birmingham men served in many regiments, four recruited strongly in Birmingham: the South Staffordshire and Worcestershire, which took men from districts which had been those counties until the city's extension in 1911; the Coldstream Guards; and the Royal Warwickshire. The 1st battalion of the Warwicks was part of the British Expeditionary Force that was rapidly deployed to France and Belgium at the start of the war. Massively outnumbered as they were yet did the British regulars show their mettle. Pushed back though they may have been, but overwhelmed they were not and at last they halted the German advance. In so doing they did the job that had been entrusted to them: they foiled the German attempt to defeat the French swiftly and end the war within weeks.

These regulars of the British Army paid a terrible price for their valour and many were killed. Amongst them was a Birmingham man who ensured that his city would play another major role in the First World War. His name was Thomas Rafferty and the assiduous research of his great nephew, John Pimm Belcher, has made it clear that Rafferty was the inspiration for the famous cartoon character 'Old Bill' created by Captain Bruce Bairnsfather who also served with the 1st battalion the Royal Warwicks. Although 'Old Bill of the better 'ole' as he became known was a humorous figure, he was a morale-boost as soldiers on the Western Front identified with him and enjoyed the cartoons of him. As the most important British cartoonist of the Great War, Bairnsfather has been recognised for his contribution to the war effort but his inspiration, Thomas Rafferty, has not. Until now. Too often academic historians fail to recognise the importance of family history research to our understanding of the past. They are mistaken to do so, for as this important work reveals, family historians can make a major contribution to historical research. John Pimm Belcher is to be congratulated on his achievement and for making clear that 'Old Bill of the Better 'Ole', belonged to Birmingham.

Professor Carl Chinn MBE, Ph.D.

Introduction

My research on 'Old Bill' started in 1990 when I began investigating my family history and I asked my mother if there was anyone of particular interest in her family. She mentioned her cousin Ivy's dad, Tom Rafferty, prompting my father to laugh "Ivy's dad was 'Corporal Jones'!", (referring to a character from the television sitcom *Dad's Army*). Mother, unamused, said that I should visit Ivy Dobbins, and so the story began. I called on Ivy and her husband Charlie at their home in Sutton Coldfield, Birmingham, where they made me welcome. Ivy recalled her mother Kate talking about Tom Rafferty – who had died on 25th April 1915 in the Second Battle of Ypres – and the fact that he had been known as 'Old Bill': also the name of a popular cartoon character of the time. My interest was sparked – what was the connection, if any, between my Great Uncle and the character of 'Old Bill'?

Mrs. Ivy Dobbins (who died in 2000 aged 87), was able to pass on photographs, newspaper cuttings and documents, dated 1914-1923, relating to her father Thomas Henry Rafferty, that had obviously been collected by his widow Kate. Upon initial inspection, it did appear that my great uncle might very well be the original inspiration for Bairnsfather's 'Old Bill', and I was keen to find out more. (To avoid confusion, whilst Ivy's married name was Dobbins, I refer to her as Ivy Rafferty throughout the text.)

Time has, though, been against my research: many of *The Old Contemptibles* of the British Expeditionary Force were lost, killed in action within a few months of the start of The Great War, whilst those who did survive came home to the Great Flu Pandemic of 1919 that claimed more lives than the war itself. To make research more difficult many official Army Records were destroyed in 1940 at the Arnside Street, Army Records Office, during the Blitz of the Second World War.

Significantly, one of the newspaper articles within Kate Rafferty's archive is titled, "The Weekly Dispatch Discovers The Original of 'Old Bill.'" Here, the Editor jubilantly declares, "Old Bill belonged to Birmingham. Bairnsfather's immortal creation once worked on a tramway-car in the Midland capital." (*The Weekly Dispatch*, 30th September 1917). In and of itself, this article constitutes a strong claim for Thomas Rafferty to be the 'original' 'Old Bill'. In addition, though – and as a result of many hours at the British Library news desk – I was gratified and excited when, in 2015, I managed to locate a slightly earlier article written by Bairnsfather himself: "Have I Insulted the British Army?", published in *The Weekly Dispatch London,* (5th August 1917). This, examined together with correspondence that Kate received from Bairnsfather, not only provided even stronger evidence that Rafferty was the inspiration for 'Old Bill', but also gave an insight into the artist's complex relationship with his creation. This book is an exploration of both Kate Rafferty's personal archive and the evidence uncovered in the course of my own research. Altogether, they have enabled me to assemble a more complete picture of Thomas and Kate Rafferty's lives.

Whilst Bairnsfather and his creation 'Old Bill' would rapidly become established within the public consciousness, Thomas Rafferty would fade from public memory – so much so that, for many years, there was no agreement over who, if anyone, was the inspiration for 'Old Bill'. I am glad to say that my own research has led to a second 'discovery' of Thomas Rafferty as the original 'Old Bill'. In this respect I am indebted to those historians who recognised the importance of my research and encouraged me in the process: Carl Chinn; Bob Bushaway; and also the Holts, the biographers of Captain Bruce Bairnsfather. Most recently *The Sunday Times* (22nd November 2015), when reporting on my research, noted the similarity between the image of Thomas Rafferty in the 'return to camp' photo, (Ill.4), with the image in the cartoon 'The Better 'Ole', (1915), (Ill.12).

The reader is invited to examine the following documentary evidence together with my accompanying narrative. My hope is that, in publishing this book, the original 'Old Bill' is not again forgotten, but retains his rightful place in history. Compiled over several years, this book charts a fascinating journey into the life and times of a remarkable man, Thomas Rafferty, and his no less remarkable wife Kate, who went on to promote his memory and raise their daughter, Ivy. Whilst there is no doubt in my own mind, I leave it up to the reader to judge for themselves who, in fact, 'Old Bill' was.

I apologise in advance if any unintentional infringement of copyright has occured, upon notification any errors will be corrected in subsequent reprints.

John Belcher

Part I

Thomas Rafferty: Birmingham's 'Old Bill'

Studio photograph of Thomas Rafferty, undated, but probably
taken to mark his marriage to Kate Howell in 1911.

1

A Biography of Thomas Rafferty

Early Life

Thomas Henry Rafferty was born on the 27th November 1884 to Samuel and Alice Rafferty at the back of house 96, Branston St, Birmingham, and was baptised on the 23rd February 1885 at St Paul's Parish Church, Birmingham. Samuel Rafferty was the son of James Rafferty, a pipe maker from Staffordshire. Samuel, Thomas's father, worked as a house painter by trade and Alice, his mother, a dressmaker. They had moved from Staffordshire to Birmingham, the 'City of a Thousand Trades', which had become prosperous through its various industries. Birmingham provided good prospects of work and plenty of accommodation, although many of its properties at this time were slums. Thomas was the fifth child of seven siblings: Alice, John, Samuel, Catherine, Will and Ada, the third youngest of four brothers.

He spent a short time in the All Saints Workhouse infirmary at the age of six, and then in his early working years was employed as a cabinet fitter and polisher until he joined the army between 1901/2, The Royal Warwickshire Regiment.

Army Service

Having joined The Royal Warwickshire Regiment, Rafferty was able to express his passion for music and become a bandsman, playing the bass drum, just as he later would with the Tramway band. By the end of his service he was to achieve the rank of Lance Corporal (Army no. 7840, 1st Battalion Royal Warwickshire Regiment). One photograph from this time shows him in full dress uniform of the 4th Battalion, together with his bass drum (Ill.3).

The Royal Warwickshire Regiment, 4th Battalion, was formed 4th January 1900, as with other battalions to supply mounted infantry for the South Africa campaign during the 2nd Boer War. However, the 4th battalion seems to have spent its time in Ireland in 1905, where they won the "Curragh Cup" at the all Ireland rifle meeting. The 4th Battalion left Ireland on 15th April

1906, and in 1907 was disbanded with Rafferty being transferred, probably to the 1st Battalion Royal Warwickshire Regiment. By this time, Thomas had evidently met Kate Howell, and they were a courting couple, demonstrated by the postcards that he sent to her – both from Bordon Camp – one on 7th June 1907, (Ill.5), and later on 10th September 1908, (Ill.4). Rafferty transferred to the reserves in 1909 (Rafferty's service with the colours would have been twelve years; seven as a regular and five as a reservist). His contemporaries in the Royal Warwickshire Regiment during those years had served in South Africa, Ireland and the North West Frontier, and whilst there is no firm documentary evidence that Rafferty himself served abroad, this remains a possibility, especially when one considers one particular photograph found within Ivy Rafferty's archive, (Ill.1).

Service with Birmingham Corporation Tramways and Marriage to Kate Howell

From 1909, Rafferty lodged at 22 Lime Grove, Venetia Road, Small Heath, Birmingham with his widowed eldest sister Alice Hanna Gillham and her future husband George Hughes, and joined the Birmingham Corporation Tramways as a motor man, playing bass drum in their band. I employed a researcher, Dr Stephen Taylor, who was able to establish dates for a number of performances referenced in the *Birmingham Tramways Gazette* by the Birmingham Corporation Military Band. We know this band met once a month through the winter, with one typical entry reading, 'Saturday 14th August 1909: performed at Sparkhill Flower Show', (Sparkhill being an inner city area of Birmingham).

Incidentally, the uniform of the tramways at that period was in the military style: a peaked hat with a large gartered badge, long service good conduct chevrons on the left hand sleeve of the jacket, insignias on the collars, and brass buttons on the jacket of the dark blue/black uniform. Rafferty would go on to be promoted to temporary inspector in 1913. Thomas Rafferty was also a literary man who kept diaries on his life experiences: these would, unfortunately, be lost when Kate passed them on to Uneeda Films, never to be returned. Thomas and his future wife Kate, worked and lived in the inner city: Kate, like many in her family, worked in the jewellery trade as a solderer and courted Thomas while he served in the army.

Thomas Rafferty married Kate Alice Howell, my Great Aunt, in 1911 at St Saviours' Church, Hockley, Birmingham. They first lived at 3 Euert Street, then at 57 Baker Street, Handsworth, Birmingham. In the October of 1912 they had their daughter, Ivy. The older members of the family that remembered Rafferty would apparently comment that he was always whistling and singing, and was somebody who was happy with his life and his lot. Rafferty was a musician who played the piano as well as the bass drum. Sadly, upon his death the re-payments on the piano could no longer be afforded, so Kate and her two sisters, Amy and Eliza, pushed it all the way back to the shop. Indeed, the return of the piano was one of my mother's main recollections of her Aunt Kate. My mother also recalled that she was a very clean and trim woman whose white apron – much like a carpenter's apron – was always white, clean and starched. Kate and her sister were allowed to keep the sweepings from the jewellery workshop where they worked, storing it in a jar until Christmas when the contents were sold to be refined into amalgam which was used in the dental trade. This money then acted as their Christmas bonus from their employer. Kate continued to live at 8 Ashleigh Place, Baker Street, Birmingham till her death on the 16th February 1953 at Western Road Hospital, Birmingham. My mother commented Kate had lived a hard life. I asked Ivy Rafferty if she had any knowledge of the extended Rafferty family but she had no information. However, in 2017, through a contact via the T H Rafferty First World War website, Lynne Taylor (née Rafferty), confirmed that at Leek in Staffordshire there were a number of relatives of Thomas Rafferty, and she herself was the granddaughter of Thomas's older brother John Rafferty.

Bruce Bairnsfather, who would become linked with Thomas Rafferty, was also a musician: as a teenager he was taught to play the banjo by his next door neighbour, a Mr. Czekacs, (Holt p.18), and also served with the Royal Warwickshire Regiments 3rd battalion before joining the Cheshire Regiment. (Whilst Rafferty was in the 1st battalion in the early 1900s, it is helpful to think of regiments as a kind of 'family' and contact between soldiers of different battalions would have occurred whilst on exercise and at military tattoos.) During this time, Bairnsfather was clearly on friendly terms with his fellow soldiers, relating, when 'under canvas' at "Wedgenock...Several of us occasionally escaped after work was over, and cleared off to Birmingham to play around and see the shows." (*Birmingham Weekly Post*, 'You Never Know, Do You?' 2nd January 1959).

Bairnsfather also joked that when, a few years later, he should have been attending evening classes on engineering at Birmingham Technical College he instead, "...took an intensive course in Higher Vaudeville at those well-known seats of learning the 'Empire', the 'Grand' and the 'Hippodrome'...I haunted the cheap seats of those good old Halls where I so often ran into 'Old Bill', his pals and his wife. The pub next door to any music Hall, anywhere, on a Saturday night was always a good place to find them." (*Birmingham Weekly Post*, 'Slithering about in Plugstreet Wood', 9th January 1959).

Quite clearly, Bairnsfather was a 'man about town' who enjoyed Birmingham's music halls not to mention the company that such establishments attracted (Holt p.21). Interestingly, we can see him here identifying 'Old Bill', not for the first time in his writings, as a 'type'. One cannot help but speculate: would Bruce and Tom have known each other during the period prior to the Great War?

Outbreak of the First World War

At the outbreak of the war in July 1914 Thomas Rafferty re-joined his Regiment, the 1st Battalion Royal Warwickshire Regiment, with immediate effect and assembled with other reservists at Shoncliffe Camp, Kent, then commanded by Colonel John Ford Elkington, part of Lieutenant-General A Haldane's Tenth Brigade. They then went north to York to join Northern Command (under General Sir Herbert Plumer), because of the apparent threat of invasion at that time to the north of England. They returned to Southampton and sailed to France on the 22nd September 1914 aboard the S.S. Caledonia. This passenger liner, belonging to the Anchor Line, was taken over as a military transport in the early part of the Great War and was large enough to carry approximately three battalions of soldiers for Boulogne, to join the British Expeditionary Force commanded by Sir John French, (*The Birmingham Weekly Dispatch*, 19th September 1914, reported 700 members of the tramways department were absent with the colours). Incidentally, Bruce Bairnsfather, who would become an inextricable part of Rafferty's story, arrived in France a couple of months later on the 29th November, according to the Medal Roll Call.

Message in a Bottle

En route to France, while passing the Isle of Wight, Rafferty – using his famed ingenuity – was to throw a bottle in the sea with a message on behalf of his comrades and himself for their wives, wishing them all well. This "novel method of communicating with one's friends" was obviously successful since the incident is recorded in *The Birmingham Daily Mail* as 'Message in a Bottle', (21st November 1914). The message was addressed to Mrs. Rafferty, 8 Hallily [Hanley] Street, Handsworth, Birmingham. (Chapter 3).

The Royal Warwickshire Regiment in France and Rafferty's shrapnel wound

The German Army had initially made strong territorial gains once it had invaded France (having violated Belgium's neutrality to get there), but lost momentum when it was defeated at the battle of the Marne (6th to 12th September 1914), and forced back to a position north of the River Aisne. Both sides then sought to turn the northern flank of their opponent in what became known as the 'Race to the Sea'.

There followed an advance by German forces that lead to the fall of Antwerp on 9th October. Haldane's brigade was consequently ordered, on the 13th October to attack the Germans at Meteren, a village in Flanders. This developed into a siege as the German forces opted to entrench themselves within the buildings. The 1st Battalion of the Royal Warwickshire Regiment, having marched out as the vanguard at 10am, attempted to drive the Germans out with guns and bayonets, and actually gained the outskirts of Meteren when they were ordered to halt at around 1pm, whilst other British forces made their advance. Meteren was captured that night, though General Haldane felt the Royal Warwickshire Regiment, having fought so valiantly, had been deprived of a victory.

Following the capture of Meteren the brigade moved slowly forward over the next five days, to Houplines on the eastern outskirts of Armentieres. It was in sight of Houplines that what we have come to know as trench warfare now became the day-to-day experience for the soldiers of the Royal Warwicks. Trench warfare was in fact the logical result of a development in arms technology that had not been matched by mobility. Trenches, therefore, provided both protection from artillery and machine guns and snipers, whilst also providing a strong defensive position from any attacking force. The development of the tank, coordinated with the rolling artillery barrage, would eventually be used by the allies to negate this defensive advantage.

Bruce Bairnsfather apparently photographed Thomas Rafferty in late 1914 giving us the 'Plugstreet Wood' photograph that would ultimately allow the public to identify him as 'Old Bill', (Part II). Kate Rafferty would later receive a copy of this photograph, probably sent by Thomas, which is how it came to be in Ivy Rafferty's possession. ('Plugstreet' was the soldiers' transliteration of the original Belgian, 'Ploegsteert'.) Incidentally, though the postal service was severely stretched by the war – with around 75,000 of its 250,000 staff being recruited over the course of the war – it still provided a remarkable service, both domestically and to the military. Rafferty, as a member of the

British Expeditionary Force was entitled to mail home for free, and mail to servicemen could be sent at the concessionary rate of 1 penny (instead of 1½ pennies). Prior to the war even small towns could receive up to 12 deliveries a day allowing parties to exchange messages over the course of a single day, and this regularity is something that persisted: we can see from Kate's correspondence with Uneeda Film Service in 1918 that Mr. I Smith mailed her the morning she was due to visit him (travelling from Birmingham to Manchester), advising her on the train times for that morning! (Chapter 11).

Sometime during 1914/1915 Rafferty was to receive a slight shrapnel wound, the metal from which he sent home to Kate to have made into a tie pin, ready for his return to England. It is possible Rafferty was slightly wounded in one of the battles within the Ypres Salient: Picardy, Albert, Artois, Bassee, Arras, Messines, Armentieres, Ysers, Ypres, Langemarck, Gheluvelt and Nonne Boschen: each one mentioned in diaries of the Royal Warwickshire Regiment. Shrapnel wounds were, of course, common and could have resulted from a minor skirmish or a German shell or sniper. Records in the battalion war diaries are sparse in detail concerning these battles: most of the old army, or *The Old Contemptibles* (those of the British Expeditionary Force who had been there since before Christmas 1914), had by this time been either killed or wounded.

It is almost certain Thomas Rafferty participated in the Christmas Truce of 1914 where soldiers of the 1st Battalion Royal Warwickshire Regiment were amongst around 100,000 British and German troops that engaged in an informal cessation of hostilities, even meeting and exchanging cigarettes and other token gifts in no-man's land. (The Pope had tried to negotiate a three day truce but this was rejected by the British Government because of German aggression two weeks earlier in the shelling of Yorkshire coastal towns.)

The Christmas Truce occurred only five months into the war and followed a lull in hostilities after the indecisive result of the first battle of Ypres. In the lead up to the week of the 25th December French, British and German soldiers in some sectors crossed over to each other's trenches to exchange gifts and seasonal greetings. On Christmas Eve and Christmas Day it is recorded that joint burial ceremonies occurred, as well as prisoner swaps and carol singing. One of the enduring images of the truce is the games of football that took place between the two sides. Bairnsfather himself recalls swapping buttons with a German officer, saying "I wouldn't have missed that unique and weird Christmas Day for anything". What makes this remarkable is the unofficial nature of this fraternisation which caused consternation amongst the command of both sides.

Indeed, the following year strongly worded statements were issued against such a repeated truce, but as the war went on the infantry became increasingly embittered anyway, and as such were less amenable to another truce.

Rafferty's Death in the Second Battle of Ypres

Not long before the second battle of Ypres we catch another glimpse of Rafferty when a short article and photograph, (Chapter 4), were published in *The Picture Post* (Friday 16th April 1915). This shows Rafferty and his pals: a 'Happy Group of Warwick's in a "Rabbit Hole" in the Trenches', (Chapter 4). It is interesting to note that Rafferty is referenced as the 'Black Hand Commander' in *The Picture Post* article, but with no further explanation as to why. Incidentally, note that Rafferty is apparently seen next to his two comrades, Biddulph and Rawlins, just as he was in the Plugstreet Wood photograph.

The British retreated after the 1st Battle of Mons and the 1st Battalion Royal Warwickshire Regiment then moved up the line (part of Major General C P Hull's Tenth Brigade that was now commanded by Lieutenant Colonel A J Poole). It was at Vielve at 4.30 am on the 25th April 1915 that the whistles were blown and the Royal Warwickshire Regiment started their advance: they got within seventy yards of the German trenches before being stopped by heavy machine gun fire. Seventeen officers and five hundred men of other ranks – including Rafferty – were killed in action during this Second Battle of Ypres. Rafferty's body was never found (or at least identified), though intriguingly Ivy referred to her father having been killed on a hill. According to the Western Front Association, killed members of the 1st Battalion Royal Warwickshire Regiment were laid to rest, side-by-side, in trenches at Meteden, Belgium, with a simple cross to mark those killed in action. However, at Tyne Cot Cemetery, Belgium, I discovered an unmarked grave to a Lance Corporal of the Royal Warwickshire Regiment, (Ill.18). I subsequently contacted the war graves commission about the possibility of carrying out a DNA check as I had located a living relative of Rafferty. This request was denied, so whilst the remains were unexamined and we will never know one way or the other, I cannot but wonder if it is indeed Rafferty's grave: 'Known Unto God'. Rafferty is, though, commemorated on The Menin Gate in Belgium.

The Regimental War Diaries state that on 25th April 1915 the German trenches were insufficiently shelled prior to the initial advance and support was unable to come up, a logistical failing that would account for the high British casualty rate. Captain Bruce Bairnsfather himself fell victim to an enemy shell during this same action in which Rafferty died, and was sent home to England with shock and hearing loss. The Second Battle of Ypres was one of the smaller battles of the First World War but nevertheless the fatality rate between April the 15th to the 2nd of May was high: 2,150 officers and 57,125 enlisted British infantry were killed in action. Notoriously, this battle would also see the first use of chlorine gas by the German Army. The Battle of St Julien on the 24th April is recorded as the worst day with 3,058 Killed In Action.

Captain Bairnsfather's creation of 'Old Bill'

Prior to the war, Bruce Bairnsfather had initially intended a career in the military and even spent time with the Royal Warwickshire Regiment and Cheshire Regiment despite having failed his military exams at Sandhurst. Ultimately, however, he left the Cheshire regiment in 1907 to train as an artist, and eventually managed to find work producing advertising sketches for the household commodities of the day: Lipton tea, Player's cigarettes, Keen's mustard, and Beecham's Pills. With the outbreak of war he joined the Royal Warwickshire Regiment as a Second Lieutenant and served with a machine gun unit.

During the Second Battle of Ypres Bairnsfather was to be invalided home with shell-shock and hearing loss, after falling victim to German artillery (Holt p.46). Shell-shock had only recently been recognised in the official literature of the time when the psychologist Charles Myers published an article describing it in *The Lancet* on 15th February 1915. At this stage in the war, whilst the British Army recognised that shell-shock was a real condition they still held an ambivalent attitude to how it should be applied. In 1915, it was instructed that, "Shell-shock and shell concussion cases should have the letter 'W' prefixed to the report of the casualty, if it was due to the enemy; in that case the patient would be entitled to rank as 'wounded' and to wear on his arm a 'wound stripe'. If, however, the man's breakdown did not follow a shell explosion, it was not thought to be 'due to the enemy', and he was to [be] labelled 'Shell-shock' or 'S' (for sickness) and was not entitled to a wound stripe or a pension." (Shephard, Ben. *A War of Nerves: Soldiers and Psychiatrists*, 1914-1994. London, Jonathan Cape, 2000). In a sense, Bairnsfather was 'fortunate' in that, having suffered hearing loss, there could be no doubt that his condition was directly due to a shell explosion.

Invalided home following the Second Battle of Ypres, Bairnsfather was posted to the 34th Division headquarters on Salisbury Plain, and it was here that the artistically gifted Captain Bruce Bairnsfather would go on to draw the popular cartoon depicting the character 'Old Bill of the Better 'Ole', (though Bairnsfather would only begin naming him as such in early 1916). In doing so it is clear that he drew upon the personalities he came to know in the frontline trenches, as Bairnsfather himself was to write in 1959, "I have so often seen and heard myself described as the creator of 'Old Bill', but the real truth is that it just somehow fell to me to notice him." (*Birmingham Weekly Post*, 2nd January 1959). Certainly, these men were very close to his heart: the dedication of his book *Bullets & Billets*, published during the war in 1917, read, "To My Old Pals, Bill, Bert, and Alf, who sat in the mud with me."

'Old Bill' was an irreverent figure who reflected the stoic humour of the brave infantryman who suffered in the trenches whilst making sardonic remarks that would have raised eyebrows at military headquarters. Indeed, in spite of his character's popularity, Bairnsfather received criticism in the House of Commons for his apparently 'vulgar caricature'. However, it was probably this irreverence that made 'Old Bill' – and by association Bairnsfather – so popular, with the latter going on to be dubbed 'the man who won the war'. Bairnsfather's cartoons were, therefore, a complex mix: 'Old Bill' was both a patriotic and affectionate portrayal of the veteran soldier, which also provided cover for indirect criticism of the establishment, and an opportunity to express the poignancy of war in sketches such as 'A Hopeless Dawn', (Ill.14). (If such a title doesn't make clear Bairnsfather's feelings, he goes on to depict a soldier despondently surveying the wreckage of a recently bombed and flooded trench.) Of particular interest is the image Bairnsfather creates in 'The Tin Opener', one of his earlier sketches where he shows us an unkempt soldier with balaclava, moustache and pipe, (Ill.13), looking for all the world just like the image of Thomas Rafferty in Bairnsfather's 'Plugstreet' photograph. Perhaps Bairnsfather's most famous sketch shows two Tommies sheltering in a shell hole in no man's land bickering about their predicament above the caption, "Well, if you knows of a better 'Ole, go to it," (Ill.12). 'Old Bill' and his 'Ole would become forever associated with Bairnsfather in the minds of the public.

Certainly, the appeal of 'Old Bill' contributed to a huge increase in sales of *The Bystander* and the boost to morale was recognised by the War Office when they gave Bairnsfather a promotion and an appointment to draw similar cartoons for other allied forces. 'Old Bill' was so popular that he quickly became a musical when, in 1917, *The Better 'Ole* opened in London at the Oxford Music Hall where it ran for over 800 performances. Post war, 'Old Bill' was to continue his popularity when a sequel *Old Bill, M.P.* (in this instance a play rather than a musical), opened at the Lyceum Theatre, London in 1922, with

Bairnsfather even appearing in it as himself. In addition, as we shall see, two silent films also called *The Better 'Ole* were made, one in 1918, and the other in 1926. 'Old Bill's' popularity would continue throughout the inter-war years, with Bairnsfather writing his autobiography *Wide Canvas*, in 1939. Perhaps inevitably, Bairnsfather became inextricably linked to his creation of 'Old Bill', but after World War II, he focused mainly on his love of landscape paintings, dying in 1959 at the age of 72.

Kate Rafferty's Correspondence with Captain Bruce Bairnsfather

Following the Second Battle of Ypres, however, Kate Rafferty was occupied with establishing her husband's well-being and whereabouts, and in this regard the letter she received from Bairnsfather's secretary is revealing, (Chapter 5). It appears she contacted Captain Bruce Bairnsfather by letter, probably around August 1915, asking for any news of her missing husband, together with photographs of him, specifically asking if he was known to Bairnsfather as 'Old Bill'. We can surmise that she sent him a copy of the 'Plugstreet' photograph for reference, and it's quite possible she wrote to Bairnsfather because of a connection that could be deduced from Rafferty's diaries and letters – and after seeing Bairnsfather's work in the press of the day, during 1915. She was probably seeking information primarily about her husband's well-being, or alternatively, some evidence by which she could claim monies on an insurance policy if Thomas had indeed been a casualty of war. After some delay (alluded to in the letter), Bairnsfather's secretary – Edward Kelly – replied to Kate's letter sympathising with her situation and confirming that there was indeed an 'Old Bill', but denying that it was Thomas Rafferty. To quote from the letter: "Captain Bairnsfather wished me to tell you it was the second and not the first man from the camera that he called 'OLD BILL' so from your letter that is not your husband as you say he was the first man near the camera."

We are left with the conundrum as to why Bruce Bairnsfather did not – at least initially – recall Rafferty as 'Old Bill'. We know that during 1916 Bruce Bairnsfather was involved in producing theatre reviews about 'Old Bill', and as public and commercial interest in Bairnsfather's work gathered pace throughout 1915, there is a suspicion that he was wary of any financial claim that Kate might have as Rafferty's widow. Certainly, this was the conclusion drawn by the editor of *John Bull*, Horatio Bottomley, who would later undertake to fight Kate Rafferty's cause. Many years later, this was also the view held by Tonie and Valmai Holt (the biographers of Bairnsfather), who observe that "out of the £100,000 profit from the stage play only £2,000 went to him[Bairnsfather]", (*The Independent*, 1992): the implication being that he was worried about seeing a reduction in his financial reward.

Intriguingly, looking back on his creation of 'Old Bill' during 1959, in the *Birmingham Weekly Post*, Bairnsfather notes that at Plugstreet, "...I was once more in the midst of the same crowd that I had mingled with at Warwick. We all lived the same sort of life, shared the same food and discomforts...", ('Walking in the mud like chimpanzees'). This familiarity with the men would seem to be very much at odds with the assertion, made by secretary Edward Kelly in the letter to Kate, where he states, "...[Bairnsfather] only saw them there once at the time he took the photograph." Later, within the same article, Bairnsfather writes, "When I looked at all the fed-up, but determined faces of the fellows round about me, heard their comments, and saw their collective resignation to such ridiculous discomfort, I inwardly laughed still more, but with the laughter of compassion. Then it was that something or other urged me to try and express some of this on paper. I began to draw again...Thus it was that 'Old Bill' started on his career. 'Old Bill' of the Warwicks and Birmingham." (Ill.11). Within the same article, Bairnsfather states, "From 'Old Bill's' point of view there was a certain amount of anxiety about the rum ration arriving, with the added worry that someone might pinch it on the way." This could, once more, be Bairnsfather referring to a 'type' of soldier, or he could indeed have meant one soldier in particular – Rafferty? But it is left ambiguous.

Kate would have needed some form of documentation to make an insurance claim with the SEID (Sheffield Equalised Independent Druids), and probably hoped Bairnsfather could provide it. Of course, by now, she had three-year-old Ivy to support, though one presumes her circumstances were better than most: her father was a boot maker and ran a newsagents shop, so it is likely he gave her financial support. Kate continued to work in the jewellery trade as she had before the Great War along with several of her family, and she may also have worked in her father's shop.

Kate would, in fact, have official confirmation of her husband's death on the 4th January 1916, from the War Office. Consequently, she would go on to receive two payments as part of the Great Gratuity Plan: £6-13s-4p on 24th April 1916, and £5 on 28th August 1919, because of the death of T H Rafferty as a Great War Casualty. The Army Pensions case file 404 of 24th January 1916 indicate that Kate Rafferty would be awarded a pension of 17s-6p. Subsequently, however, the Army Pensions register (revised version), of 26th May 1930 records that on 16th July 1920 Kate Rafferty was awarded an increased widows pension of 26s-8p per week, and 10s per week for her daughter Ivy. The same records show that, from 1930, Kate was receiving a widows pension of 44s-11p.

Bairnsfather Identifies Thomas Rafferty as the Original 'Old Bill'

In spite of what Bairnsfather might have claimed in his letter to Kate, my discovery at the British Library during 2015 threw an entirely different light on the subject. The article I uncovered was written by Bairnsfather himself and titled 'Have I insulted the British Army?', (*Weekly Dispatch London*, 5th August 1917). Without mentioning Rafferty by name, Bairnsfather did in fact identify him, by way of a photograph, as the inspiration for 'Old Bill'. This photograph was taken in the vicinity of Plugstreet Wood, in 1914, by Bairnsfather, and also featured the 'original' Alf and Bert. From the text it appears Bairnsfather was stung into the publication of the 'Plugstreet' photograph after he was accused within The Times Literary Supplement of 21st December 1916, 'The Soldier that made the Empire Laugh', for his portrayal of the troops as a dishevelled and ill-mannered rabble.

With an excitement that must have echoed that of Kate Rafferty's many years before, I of course recognised it as the same, (cropped), 'Plugstreet Wood' photograph within Kate's collection, (Part II). In publishing this photograph Bairnsfather wanted to prove that these men really did look as 'disreputable' as he depicted them, but contrasted this with their 'virtues' and 'valour'. Indeed, he was so keen to prove that his creation was based in fact that he named the figures in his photograph 'Alf', 'Bert', and 'Old Bill' (though without disclosing their actual names). The accompanying text reads: "I have invented nothing. This photograph I took in Plug-street Wood in 1914, and here you see for the first time the originals of Old Bill, Bert, and Alf as I knew them and portrayed them." Significantly, for our purposes, the image of Rafferty is clearly labelled as 'Old Bill'. (Chapter 5).

This photograph no doubt prompted a great deal of local interest amongst the populace of Birmingham – and most likely – from Kate Rafferty herself who, one guesses, was insistent that the truth of her late husband's identity be known to the wider public. Eventually, as can be seen from the cuttings that Kate kept, on 30th September 1917, *The Weekly Dispatch London* would explicitly identify Thomas Rafferty as 'Old Bill' in their article, "The Weekly Dispatch Discovers The Original of 'Old Bill'." Apparently, such was the groundswell of public opinion, '...it need only be said that the identification of Rafferty as Old

Bill came through the publication of the photograph of Bairnsfather's hero in *The Weekly Dispatch*. His friends saw it and immediately exclaimed: "That's Pat Rafferty." (ibid.). The newspaper even features two contrasting images of Thomas Rafferty (presumably supplied by Kate), taken before and during the war. The caption reads: *"How war transforms the man"*. (Chapter 8).

The Birmingham Daily Mail would publish a similar article on the 1st October naming Thomas Henry Rafferty as 'Old Bill': "Handsworth Original of a Bairnsfather Hero." (Chapter 9).

These articles are keen to point out Rafferty's unique flare and initiative that made him stand out amongst his work-mates, and it is the closest we get (with the loss of his diaries), to the words of the man himself. Upon the outbreak of war he is said to have proclaimed: "'So long boys, we'll soon have this job over, and then I'll be with you again'...He smiled at the idea of the Germans, 'miserable, under-fed blighters,' as he conceived them, standing up to a regiment of British Regulars...At the depot it was Rafferty's merry voice: 'Well, now, whose call is it?' which inevitably prefaced a spell of conviviality, for even in these things he led the way." (*The Weekly Dispatch London* 30th September 1917).

The Original 'Alf' and 'Bert'

It is right that the possible identities of the original 'Alf' and 'Bert' should also receive some scrutiny. Comparing the faces on the 'Plugstreet' photograph, (Part II), with that of the named figures in *The Picture Post* of the 'Happy group of Warwicks', (Chapter 4), William Biddulph "the Stoker" bears a likeness to 'Bert', whilst it is possible that – somewhat confusingly – Bert Rawlins "the chef" was 'Alf'.

William Biddulph is, in fact, well documented in the book *North West Frontier 1908* by Peter Duckers, (2006 p.90). Biddulph, army no. 6779 enlisted with the Royal Warwickshire Regiment on 1st May 1899 at the age of nineteen and became a signaller. He served in The Boer Wars achieving the rank of L/Cpl and also served on the North West Frontier in the Zakka Khel and Mohmand campaigns. He was invalided back to England on the 29th October 1908, suffering with enteric fever (known now as typhoid fever). Biddulph rejoined the Royal Warwickshire Regiment 1st Battalion in 1914 and suffered a bullet wound to his left arm at the Battle of Ypres on the 25th April 1915. He was discharged, unfit for duty, and awarded the Silver War badge no. 16791. From previous campaigns he had been awarded the Queens South Africa Medal; King's South Africa Medal with clasps for Cape Colony, Orange Free State and

Transvaal; the India General Service Medal with North West Frontier clasp 1908. His decorations from The Great War were: The 1914 Mons Star; War Medal; and Victory Medal. He was finally discharged on the 8th May 1916.

If 'Alf' is indeed Bert Rawlins, despite his war records being lost we can establish the following from census information. From the 1901 census, aged 19, he would have served at Colchester Garrison 3, army no. 7262. From the 1911 census we learn that he married Marion Beaumont in 1910 and they lived at Swan Lane, Coventry, during which time Rawlins apparently worked as a blacksmith. From the First World War Pension Ledgers and index cards that record his death on 25th April 1914, we learn they had three children: Marion, Florence and Bertram. He was decorated with the 1914 Mons Star and Victory Medal. Like Rafferty, he is commemorated on The Menin Gate.

Kate Rafferty's Communication with Horatio Bottomley, Collaboration with Uneeda Film Service, and the loss of Thomas Rafferty's Diaries

We can see from Kate's archive that she must have been in correspondence with Horatio Bottomley, the editor of *John Bull*, a populist weekly newspaper. Bottomley was a garrulous figure of the age, who, having spent time in an orphanage went on to become a financier and MP for Hackney South. In 1912 he had to resign from Parliament after he was declared bankrupt, but saw a revival in his fortunes with the outbreak of WWI, becoming a prominent propagandist for the war effort – even at one stage being touted as a possible member of the war cabinet. When Kate Rafferty contacted him, she would have done so because at the time Bottomley was considered the friend of the returning soldier and 'The People's Hero'. Indeed, Bottomley was vigorous in supporting Kate's cause when, on October 5th 1918, he publicly wrote within the letter pages of *John Bull* that, having made a great deal of money out of sketching Rafferty Bairnsfather might, 'make arrangements...to give her [Kate] a handsome pension?' (Chapter 10). Needless to say, such public admonishments must have made uncomfortable reading for Bairnsfather.

Someone else who contacted Bottomley during 1918 was Mr. I Smith of Uneeda Film Service concerning an article about Thomas Rafferty that had been published within the pages of *John Bull*. (Uneeda Film Service of Deansgate, Manchester, were the official agents for Topical Budget, under the supervision of The Ministry of Information: at the time Manchester was a creative centre for the burgeoning film industry). Mr. I Smith then went on to contact Kate Rafferty, having been directed to her by Bottomley, proposing that they make a film about her husband's life and experiences in the army. It seems Kate was very much in agreement because she went on to meet with a writer in Manchester and then sent Mr. I Smith four diaries written by her husband Thomas Rafferty, and a contract was subsequently signed by both parties, (Chapter 11). Unfortunately for Kate, Mr. I Smith was to disappear along with these diaries. It seems the last Kate heard from him was when he sent her a letter on January 18th 1919 saying he was travelling to America for a short time and was leaving things in the hands of one of his partners, a W Millward of the Cinema Club Ormes Buildings, the Parsonage Manchester. This must have been excruciating for Kate who would have had to reconcile herself with the fact that the film – and any payments attached to it – would not, now, be made. Not only this, but she had handed over her husband's diaries which, aside from their sentimental value, no doubt contained proof of the fact that he was 'Old Bill'. Kate's consternation is evidenced by the fact that she went on to contact Horatio Bottomley in April 1918 who investigated her troubles without success, (Chapter 13). Many years later, in 2015, I too was notified that there was no such record of a 'Uneeda Film Service' when I contacted Companies House.

Kate Rafferty is Publicly Acknowledged as the Wife of 'Old Bill'

Uneeda Film Service never made their proposed film (instead going bankrupt), but before Mr. I Smith's disappearance, we can see from the correspondence that Kate's presence was requested "on Friday evening at the Palladium [20th December 1918] when we hope to present you with a substantial amount." (Chapter 11). This ties in neatly with an advertisement in the *Manchester Evening Chronicle*, on the 20th December, which announces: "Mrs. Rafferty, wife of the late T Rafferty 'OLD BILL' will be presented by the Management with a Purse of Treasury Notes, which has been subscribed by the Management and the Audience this week when showing the Film featuring her late Husband 'THE BETTER OLE'". Similarly, advertisements in both the *Manchester Evening Chronicle* and *Manchester Evening News* earlier that week also reference Kate's forthcoming appearance, (Chapter 12). (Having contacted Manchester City Council in 1991 it was a researcher at Manchester Central Library who helped me locate the adverts concerning Kate Rafferty's appearance at Manchester Palladium).

Though not referenced in either the correspondence or the adverts, it appears that Kate was also presented with a Commemorative Peace medal at this performance (Ill.15). Certainly, Ivy believed that this was how her mother came to be in possession of it, though she did not recall her mother talking in any detail about her stage appearance. After much research I located only one other such Peace medal, in the British Museum medal collection, indicating that these were limited items, commissioned for presentation. Peace medals were a way of marking the end of conflict (hence their name), and were typically presented to children, many of them throughout 1919. For Kate to have such a medal so soon after the end of the war indicates how rapidly the decision to produce them was made.

The film, *The Better 'Ole*, made by the production company Welsh and Pearson premiered at the Alhambra, Leicester Square, London, on the 22nd April 1918, and became a commercial success. Incidentally, T A Welsh had been showing news reels in France for The British Ministry of Information, but returned home specifically to make a film about 'Old Bill'. It appears that Uneeda Film Service had not been the only company actively leveraging the commercial potential of the 'Old Bill' 'franchise'.

Whilst the cinema was still in its infancy, the music hall and their associated stars were the traditional and dominant form of entertainment. During the First World War they played an important role in drumming up support for the war, both encouraging young men to enlist and raising morale as these same men continued to die in ever greater numbers as the war progressed.

One such performer was Gertie Gitana who has become known by some historians as the Dame Vera Lynn of the First World War, given her popularity with the front-line troops. She had been recording songs since 1910 so was well known by the start of the war. She would perform for wounded soldiers in hospital and have signings where she would raise funds for the war effort, and the soldiers themselves. Her popularity was signalled by the fact that the soldiers would often alter the lyrics to her songs.

Another popular performer was Vesta Tilley who worked as a male impersonator before the war, and then dressed as a soldier during the war. Performing in the guise of such characters as 'Tommy of the Trenches', she actively recruited during her shows, as Kitty Morter later recalled when, on a night out to Manchester's Palace Theatre in 1914, Tilley recruited her husband. "She [Vesta] introduced that song 'We don't want to lose you but we think you ought to go'... She came out of the stage and walked all around in the audience. She put her hand on my husband's shoulder and as the men were all following her down, he got up and followed her down too and they all went on the stage. I was so very proud that he...was going to be soldier." He would not, however, survive the war and would leave Kitty a widow with a young child, an experience that echoed that of Kate Rafferty. Tragically, this must have been an all too common occurrence.

However, surprising as it may seem, there was still room for nuance and irony within their performances. These were, after all, sophisticated and seasoned performers who understood the tragedy that many of their audience had experienced, and songs were often performed in a knowing and sceptical way that allowed the audience to jeer at the form of patriotism presented to them.

This combination of scepticism and escapism was readily apparent in the cartoons of 'Old Bill', and it was perhaps only a matter of time before the character was to make his debut on the stage, and later cinema. Billy Russell, who had been performing on stage whilst still a child adopted the persona of 'Old Bill' to entertain his fellow troops of the South Staffordshire Regiment, with whom he served during WWI. Following the war, with Bairnsfather's endorsement, he continued to perform as 'Old Bill', except that – realising that many didn't want to be reminded of war – he modified his act, renaming it 'Old Bill in Civvies'.

In 1926 another film, also entitled *The Better 'Ole*, was released in America portraying Syd Chaplin (Charlie Chaplin's brother) as 'Old Bill'. At one point, the character is portrayed prostrate in a large bass drum and appears to have a wound strip on his blouson cuff. In fact, this echoed the real life experience of Rafferty who played the bass drum and had also been wounded.

'Old Bill's' popularity would prove to be remarkably long-lasting: in 1941, during the Second World War, he would be brought back for a morale boosting film, *Old Bill and Son*. This film, partly scripted by Bairnsfather himself, features 'Old Bill' as a veteran soldier of World War I in various comedic situations with his son, both having signed up to serve their country.

In 1928 Kate Rafferty, with the help of a private detective Mr. George Fergus McDonald, Justice of the Peace of 263 Grove Lane, Handsworth, Birmingham, tried to trace the pals of her deceased husband without success. It is unclear precisely what prompted Kate to do this. As we have seen she had already received the public acknowledgement that Rafferty was 'Old Bill', but it is reasonable to believe that she was seeking further proof that this was indeed the case. Aside from this, she may simply have wanted to speak with comrades who had been close to Thomas and reminisce about old times.

T H Rafferty's Comrades in the Royal Warwickshire Regiment

The nine soldiers of the Royal Warwick's 1st battalion named alongside Rafferty in the newspaper articles used in research for this book were: William Biddulph, Henry Revill, F Hubbal, J Scott, Charles Lapham, Bert Rawlins, William Roberts, S Rollins and George Owen. (The presumption must be they were identified as such by Captain Bairnsfather who had actually served with them.) Six of these men were killed in action, four on the same day as Rafferty. Private William Biddulph was wounded by a bullet in his left arm and was medically discharged under Kings Regulations (18th May 1916) whilst Privates J Scott and S Rollins went on to survive the Great War. They all received the 1914 Mons Star.

The son of Private S Rollins, Cyril B Rollins, confirmed that his father knew Rafferty as 'Old Bill' and also gave me a photograph of the Royal Warwickshire Band showing his father and Rafferty, (Ill.2). Private S Rollins was present at the Christmas Truce and went on to serve with the Royal Warwick's becoming a Sergeant at Tidworth Barracks Wiltshire. Here he played the clarinet alongside his cousin Alf Jarvis who played the trombone in the Royal Warwickshire Band.

The Contenders for the Origin of 'Old Bill'

Previously, the most convincing argument against any single person being the original inspiring figure for 'Old Bill' has been that he was really just a 'type' of soldier – a universal personality that was particularly prominent amongst the *Old Contemptibles*. As time wore on it does seem that Bairnsfather had created an archetypal figure – rooted in a certain time and place – but one that many were keen to play up to. For instance, the *Birmingham Weekly Post* (2nd October 1959), that carries Bairnsfather's obituary, notes: "Many people claimed to be the original 'Old Bill' model, including a walrus-moustached soldier from the Warwickshire Regt. who died, a Chelsea pensioner, in 1941...", though here he goes unnamed.

Private Godley of the 4th Battalion Royal Fusiliers was certainly one candidate for the original 'Old Bill' model. He fought courageously, single-handedly manning a machine gun to defend Nimy bridge during the battle of the Mons when the commanding officer, Lieutenant Dease, was mortally wounded. Both Godley and Dease (posthumously), would receive the Victoria Cross for their selfless actions. Indeed, it was probably his undoubted courage that elevated him to the status of being a possible candidate for 'Old Bill' in the minds of many. Private Godley was to survive the war and actually used to dress up as 'Old Bill' when raising money for service charities, his image complete with bushy moustache and pipe. As such, he even acquired the nickname 'Old Bill', so it is no surprise that many in the past believed him to be the 'original'.

Still, Bairnsfather would throughout later life maintain there was no single model for 'Old Bill', and it is of course reasonable to believe that he, like all artists, drew on a variety of different people and situations for inspiration. In the *Coventry Evening Telegraph*, 15th May 1957, Brigadier C T Tomes was quoted as saying "As

I served with Bruce Bairnsfather in the trenches when these sketches were first drawn, I think I am right in saying that there was no particular model. 'Old Bill' was just a type of the older reservist who had been called up at the outbreak of war," (quoted within *The Antelope*, the journal of the Royal Warwickshire Regiment). Again, however, we return to Bairnsfather's article, "Have I insulted the British Army?", and the 'Plugstreet' photo. Here, Rafferty's image is clearly labelled as 'Old Bill', and indeed described in the text as the 'original'. So, whilst Bairnsfather's caricature may well have given life to an enduring and instantly recognisable 'type' that would take inspiration from many different people, the fact that Thomas Rafferty was the original inspiration for 'Old Bill' appears unequivocal.

Why 'Old Bill'?

The Birmingham newspaper, *The Weekly Dispatch*, 30th September 1917, mentions that Rafferty was known locally as 'Pat' Rafferty, rather than 'Old Bill', indicating that he gained this nickname once he had returned to the Army. Captain Bairnsfather himself refers to the original 'Old Bill', implying that a man with that nickname was already in existence – and was not his invention. But why 'Old Bill'?

There is much speculation as to why the police were called the 'Old Bill', and whilst I do not seek to offer a definitive explanation as to the origin of the phrase, the connection between this sobriquet and our 'Old Bill' demands attention. Within their biography of Bairnsfather the Holts mention that on 20th August 1919 in the magazine, *Fragments*, Bairnsfather announced the 'Old Bill Double' Competition to find the ex-soldier who most fully matched the character of 'Old Bill', with the winner being entitled to £5 a week for a year. The winner, announced on 11th October, was Samuel Birkenshaw who happened to be an ex-policeman. The implication is, of course, that the term 'Old Bill' consequently fell into common parlance for describing policemen. If this is indeed the origin of the term 'Old Bill' for the police then one must reasonably assume that they were not known as such before this time. However, it is worth noting that the dress uniform of the Royal Warwickshire Regiment (complete with peaked helmet), was not unlike a police officer's uniform of the time, (see Ill.3). (In this respect, there is at least circumstantial evidence that Rafferty could have been named after the slang term 'Old Bill' because of his dress uniform, if indeed the term was already in circulation). This is the uniform that Rafferty would have worn when playing his bass drum and which he apparently became associated with, both in civilian and army life:

one newspaper article commenting, "His instrument was the big drum, no doubt chosen because it made the most noise and set our hero apart from the rest." (*Birmingham Daily Mail*, 'Handsworth Original Of Bairnsfather Hero', 1917). If the term 'Old Bill' for police was already in circulation it would only be a small leap of imagination for it to come into common parlance amongst members of the Regiment for Thomas Rafferty. Given the popularity of the 'Old Bill' caricature following the war it is quite possible that the term then became synonymous with the stereotypical image of a policeman, whether or not the term 'Old Bill' had already been in circulation before the war.

With regard to Regimental band performances, they were probably a more regular occurrence before their transportation to France, given both the chaos of the frontline and the casualty rate of men either invalided or killed in action, which would ultimately have made the bands unviable. In quieter periods the troops would have entertained themselves instead with alternatives such as boxing or football. The Regimental War Diary of the 16th April 1915 reads: "Training. Played Seaforths at football, won 4-0. Glorious weather." (Incidentally, the Seaforths – a Scottish Regiment – were one of those that are known to have played football with the Germans during the Christmas Truce, in their case against the 133rd Royal Saxon Regiment: the score on that occasion was 3-2 to the Germans.)

As to the dress uniform of the day, the line regiment's tunic was red with blue trousers; the India uniform was Blue for Winter and White for Summer; and the men also wore the Hindustani colour called Khaki. In 1906 The First Volunteer Battalion Royal Warwickshire Regiment's uniform was all blue with red piping that looked similar to a police officer's uniform. At concert parties or similar engagements the band may have worn non-standard dress uniforms or even costumes.

Brothers' War Service and Decoration

Rafferty's brothers all fought – and survived – the First World War. Indeed, his elder brother John had previously enlisted in March 1902, and it's possible that Thomas was inspired to join the army around the same time because of this. John was to embark for France with the 1st Battalion King's Royal Rifles on the 28th August 1914 and was awarded The Mons Star, War and Peace medals. Rafferty's other elder brother Samuel served with the Royal Warwickshire Regiment army (no. 1562) between 4th May 1915 till 4th August 1916 (and was awarded the 1915 Star, British War medal and Peace medal and the UK silver war service badge). Samuel was eventually discharged as medically unfit for duty. Rafferty's youngest brother William enlisted with the Royal Warwickshire Regiment in 1914 and served with The Royal Fusiliers and the Labour Core, and was awarded The 1915 Star, War and Peace Medals.

Thomas Rafferty's own medals include; The 1914 Mons Star and Clasp, issued on 24th June 1919; The British War Medal and The Victory Medal, issued together in 1919, (Ill.15). The 1914 Mons Star and Clasp were instituted in 1917 and awarded to those under fire or in range of the enemies' guns between 5th August 1914 till November 1914. This information was recorded on medical cards and medal index cards so the medals would automatically be issued to the next of kin of those 'killed in action'. We also have War Office documents relating to Rafferty's death, (Ill.17); a letter from King George V, (Ill.16), that would have accompanied the now missing Death Plaque, (Ill.19), issued in 1918; and a Commemorative scroll issued in 1919, (Part III). We can also draw upon information within the Army Register of Soldiers' Effects, (which detailed money owed to men who died in service). With Rafferty's medals there was also The Peace medal which was apparently presented to Kate Rafferty at her appearance at the Manchester Palladium, (Ill.15). As noted earlier, I located only one other such Commemorative Peace medal in the British Museum medal collection, indicating that these medals were limited items, commissioned for presentation.

Memorials

There is a large Transport Ground War Memorial at Billesley, Birmingham which was dedicated on the 28th May 1922 to the transport workers who gave their lives in the First World War – Rafferty is commemorated on this memorial along with other employees from the Hockley Depot, (Ill.20). This memorial was paid for by the members of the Tramways Social Club branches with a weekly levy of one pence a week. (Further information is recorded in the book *From Trams to Trenches: the story of Birmingham Corporation Tramways workers who gave their lives in the First World War*, by Douglas H Smith MBE, on behalf of the National Express Bus company). Alongside Rafferty, other named soldiers that died serving with the 1st Battalion Royal Warwickshire Regiment were Privates Arthur Taylor, Robert Neal, Henry Brice, George Beale, George Gilbert, *Thomas Lewis, *Arthur Phillips, *Bertram Walker, Frank Hastings, James Edwards, Peter Smith, John Baker, Robert Merrick, Lance Corporal Thomas Spencer and Sergeant Percy Weeks (those marked with asterisks were killed in action on the same day as Rafferty).

A friend of mine, Robert Betteridge who did some research on my behalf, concluded that there were memorial plaques at Hockley tramway depot dedicated to those who had worked there and lost their lives in the First World War. However, it could not be located, so it probably vanished when the Hockley depot was demolished and the building suppliers Travis Perkins took over the land. Unfortunately, unlike today, memorials then did not have to be registered.

Rafferty's name is also on a memorial to the Royal Warwickshire and the Staffordshire Regiments commemorating soldiers killed in action at the Church of God, Seventh Day, Grove Lane, Handsworth. (In 1914 this was known as St Peter's parish church). This is dated 1923 and was dedicated on Sunday the 26th December 1936 to those who lost their lives in the First World War who were members of that parish. Coincidentally, the Raffertys would have lived just round the corner from this very church.

Conclusion

To summarise, the weight of evidence – that Thomas Rafferty was indeed the inspiration for 'Old Bill' – would appear to be beyond reasonable doubt. My research, laid out in these pages, has been vindicated by Tonie and Valmai Holt, the biographers of Bruce Bairnsfather, as well as several other military historians. In the future, my hope is that this book will stimulate further research into Rafferty and provide us with an even fuller picture of this flamboyant man. I would never have expected to come across the article written by Bairnsfather, 'Have I Insulted the British Army', which would be instrumental in proving Rafferty was the original 'Old Bill'. Who knows, perhaps Thomas Rafferty's diaries will also, one day, be discovered and what a mine of information that would be! My intention here, though, has been to not only demonstrate the validity of his claim to be the original 'Old Bill', but to give the reader an insight into his character, and also that of his wife who would go on to promote his memory and

raise their only child, Ivy, who – many years later – provided me with much of the evidence that I have explored here.

Photograph showing mother and daughter, Ivy and Kate Rafferty, together at Ivy and Charlie's home at Rough road, Kingstanding, Birmingham. Undated, but circa late 1940s – early 1950s?

1. Camp photograph at an unknown location, possibly South Africa. It is undated, but is possibly from Thomas Rafferty's early service in the Boer War, circa 1902. It shows Thomas Rafferty, top row second from left, with fellow soldiers. It is not clear what is happening but there appears to be a great deal of hilarity surrounding the fact that most men are posing with chickens for some unknown reason. Adding to the theatricality of the scene, the man to the right of Rafferty appears to be wearing a top hat.

2. The son of S Rollins, Cyril Rollins, gave me this photograph of the Regimental band of the 4th Battalion, (disbanded in 1907), so it was probably taken circa 1904/5, possibly at Budbrooke Barracks in Warwickshire. S Rollins is third row down on the left, marked with an 'x'. Rafferty is in the centre of the front row with his bass drum. The conductor was apparently known as 'The Blue Flash'.

3. A splendid photograph of bandsman Rafferty in full dress uniform with his bass drum. This photograph shows Rafferty in the dress uniform of the 4th Battalion. It was disbanded in 1907 and he was then transferred to the 1st Battalion, so this photograph can be no later than 1907, and probably circa 1906. (Note that the 'apron' worn by Rafferty in this photograph would have been made from the skin of an antelope, part of the insignia of the R.W.R.).

4. Bordon Camp, 1908. A postcard, (dated 10th September, 1908), sent by Thomas Rafferty to Kate from Bordon Camp. Thomas is in the front row, fourth from left.

5. Bordon Camp, 1907. A postcard, (dated 7th June, 1907), sent by Thomas Rafferty to Kate Howell when they were a courting couple. Taken at Bordon Camp, Hampshire, it shows men of the 1st Battalion of Royal Warwickshire Regiment with Rafferty holding the broom standing at the back of the snowman.

6. Studio photograph of Kate Rafferty (1911).

7. Sentimental card kept by Kate Rafferty, presumably prompted by her husband's re-joining of his old Regiment at the outbreak of WWI, in 1914.

8. Studio photograph of Ivy Rafferty at 3 years of age (1915).

9. Bandsman Rafferty, (left), with a fellow drummer, presumably taken at the same time as plate 3 (1906). His fellow bandsman on the right is posing with a snare drum.

10. An undated photograph showing Thomas Rafferty on the left, with two other fellow cyclists. It is most likely toward the end of his first period of service, circa 1908/1909.

11. Bairnsfather's sketch of 'Old Bill' with the badge of the Royal Warwickshire Regiment that shows an antelope with a coronet around its neck linked to a chain wrapped around the animal's body, circumstantial evidence of the link between the artist and Rafferty who shared the same regiment (unknown date).

12. 'The Better 'Ole'. Perhaps Bairnsfather's most famous sketch, it demonstrates the stoicism and humour of the British soldier amidst the terror of an artillery barrage. Note the facial similarity of the character on the right to the photographs of Thomas Rafferty (1915). Courtesy of Tonie and Valmai Holt.

13. 'The Tin Opener'. An early sketch by Bairnsfather, possibly of Thomas Rafferty, which would go on to inform his creation of 'Old Bill' (1915).

14. 'A Hopeless Dawn'. This sketch, notably devoid of any humour, (stoic or otherwise), arguably demonstrates the 'anti-war' aspect of Bairnsfather's work (1916).

15. Top: Thomas Rafferty's cap badge. Middle, left: Mons Star with bar '1914'. Centre: Silvery British War Medal. Right: Victory medal. Bottom: Commemorative Peace Medal issued to Kate Rafferty, (on the reverse are three English Lions). This was presented to Kate Rafferty on 20th December 1918 on stage at the Manchester Palladium where she was publicly recognised as the wife of 'Old Bill'.

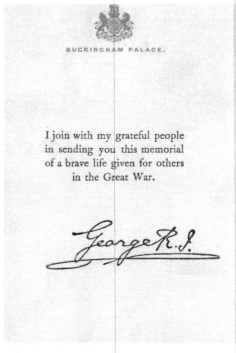

BUCKINGHAM PALACE.

I join with my grateful people in sending you this memorial of a brave life given for others in the Great War.

George R.I.

16. A 'signed' letter from George V that would have accompanied the Commemorative Plaque of Thomas Rafferty, (Ill.23).

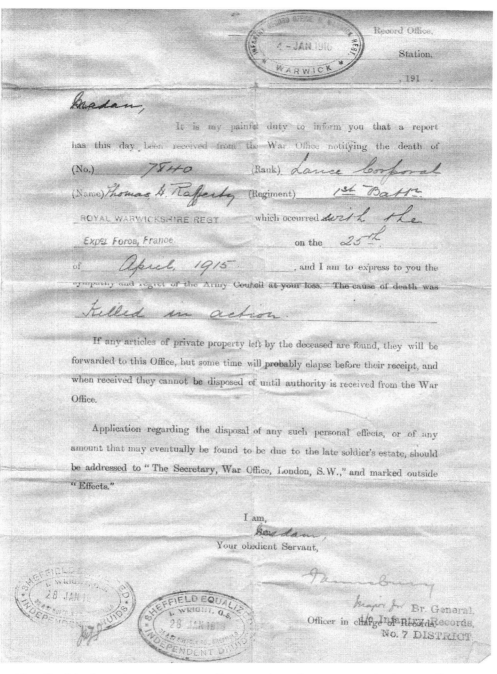

Record Office,

Station,

, 191 .

Madam,

It is my painful duty to inform you that a report has this day been received from the War Office notifying the death of

(No.) 78440 (Rank) *Lance Corporal*

(Name) *Thomas H. Rafferty* (Regiment) *1st Battn.*

ROYAL WARWICKSHIRE REGT which occurred *with the*

Expn. Force, France. on the *25th*

of *April, 1915* , and I am to express to you the sympathy and regret of the Army Council at your loss. The cause of death was

Killed in action.

If any articles of private property left by the deceased are found, they will be forwarded to this Office, but some time will probably elapse before their receipt, and when received they cannot be disposed of until authority is received from the War Office.

Application regarding the disposal of any such personal effects, or of any amount that may eventually be found to be due to the late soldier's estate, should be addressed to "The Secretary, War Office, London, S.W.," and marked outside "Effects."

I am,

Madam,

Your obedient Servant,

Major for Br. General,

Officer in charge of Records,

No. 7 DISTRICT

17. The official death certificate of Thomas Rafferty, issued on 4th January 1916, by the War Office. (Note the stamp of the 'Sheffield Independent Equalized Druids' insurance company, dated 28th January 1916, signifying that she had provided this as proof of her husband's death in order to make her claim).

18. The gravestone of the unknown Lance Corporal of the R.W.R. It remains a possibility that this is the final resting place of Thomas Rafferty, though we should note that Rafferty was killed in April 1915 and Tyne Cot cemetery began in October 1917. To have justified a grave any bodily remains that survived must have been relatively substantial.

19. Replica Death plaque of Thomas Rafferty, issued in 1918.

20. Transport Ground War Memorial at Billesley, Birmingham which was dedicated on the 28th May 1922 to the transport workers who gave their lives in the Great War – Rafferty is commemorated on this memorial along with other employees from the Hockley Depot.

2

Thomas Rafferty: Timeline

1884

27th Nov   Born to Samuel and Alice Rafferty in the back of a house in Branston Street, Birmingham.

1891   Resident at 8 Court, 2 House, St Georges, Birmingham.

1901   Resident at 14 Court, 3 House, New Summer Street, Birmingham. Thomas was one of seven children, and at the age of 6 is recorded as spending a short time in the workhouse infirmary.

1901-1903   Employed as a cabinet fitter and polisher.

1903-1909   Thomas does army service with the Royal Warwickshire Regiment, playing bass drum in the regimental band. He will go on to ultimately achieve the rank of Lance Corporal.

1907   Courts Kate Howell, a jewellery solderer by trade.

7th Jun   Posts a card to Kate Howell from Bordon Camp, (Ill.5).

9th Feb   The 4th Royal Warwickshire Regiment battalion is formally disbanded. Thomas Rafferty is then transferred to the 1st battalion.

1908

Dec   Thomas's mother Alice dies in Western Road Infirmary aged 52.

10th Sep	Posts a card to Kate from Bordon Camp, informing her they are returning to Lichfield Barracks, (Ill.4).
1909-1914	Transfers to the Royal Warwickshire Regiment reserves.
1909	Thomas joins the Birmingham Corporation Tramways as a motor man. He plays the bass drum in the tramways band.
1911	
Jan-Feb	Thomas's father Samuel dies in the Aston Union Firmary aged 61. (He never witnesses his son's marriage to Kate Howell.)
29th Oct	Thomas marries Kate at St Saviours Church, Hockley, Handsworth, Birmingham. It is likely that this is when Thomas and Kate have studio photographs taken, to mark the event, (Ill.6 & front cover). (Thomas's photograph, which was coloured, was taken by Hudson & Co, Western Arcade, Birmingham. Kate's photograph by Hamnett's, 197 Bristol Road, Birmingham. One might have expected a photograph of them together, but, if there ever was one, it was not amongst Ivy Rafferty's collection).
1912	
14th Oct	Ivy Irene Rafferty born to Kate and Thomas Rafferty.
1914	
4th Aug	Britain declares war on Germany after they invade Belgium. Rafferty re-joins his regiment, the 1st Battalion Royal Warwickshire Regiment.
22nd Sep	Sails to France in the S.S. Caledonia.
21st Nov	Newspaper article, 'Message in a Bottle', published by *The Birmingham Daily Mail* that references Thomas Rafferty.

Dec	Photograph taken by Bruce Bairnsfather of Thomas Rafferty in the trenches at Ploegsteert Wood, (Part II). A copy was subsequently sent to Kate Rafferty, probably by Thomas. (Mounted by H Greenfield, 342 Soho Road, Handsworth, Birmingham. There is another address on the mounting rear G H Anderton, 110 Alfred Road, Handsworth, Birmingham).
24th-26th Dec	The Christmas Truce, which amongst others, involves the 1st Battalion Royal Warwickshire Regiment.
1914-1915	Thomas is slightly wounded by shrapnel. He sends this piece of shrapnel home to Kate to have made into a tie pin on his return to England.
1915	
14th Apr	A picture of Rafferty in *The Picture Post*, called 'Happy Group of Warwick's in a "Rabbit Hole" in the Trenches' (Chapter 4).
25th Apr	Thomas Rafferty is killed in action at The 2nd Battle of Ypres. Bruce Bairnsfather also participates in this battle and is sent home with shell-shock.
30th Aug	A letter from Bruce Bairnsfather in reply to Kate's enquiry about news of her husband. Bairnsfather maintains he did not know Rafferty as 'Old Bill', but rather one of his companions instead, in an apparent act of deliberate misdirection.
late 1915?	Photograph, undated, but it shows Ivy Rafferty at about age three, (Ill.8).
1916	
4th Jan	Kate receives the death certificate of Thomas Rafferty, (Ill.17). This would subsequently entitle her to his service gratuity.

Jan | Kate Rafferty contacts the Sheffield Equalised Independent Druids sending proof her husband has been killed in action. (The SEID was instituted as a friendly society in 1858. The Sheffield District had 84 Lodges, the strongest in England. It was a mutual society association for the purpose of insurance, pensions and savings, a benefit society with Masonic Links). Kate received her official war office documents back from SEID on January 1916 with the official stamp of the SEID.

24th Apr | Kate receives her first War Gratuity payment of £6-13s-4p.

21st Dec | *The Times Literary Supplement* 'The Soldier That Made The Empire Laugh' accuses Bairnsfather of depicting British soldiers in the form of a 'cruel caricature'.

1917

5th Aug | *The Weekly Dispatch* (London), publishes 'Have I Insulted the British Army', by Bruce Bairnsfather. It is written in direct response to the article in The Times, and is the first and apparently only time that Bairnsfather readily identifies 'Old Bill' by publishing his photograph of Plugstreet Wood, featuring Thomas Rafferty and his companions.

30th Sep | *The Weekly Dispatch* publishes the article 'The Weekly Dispatch Discovers The Original of 'Old Bill''. In response to Bairnsfather's article, Thomas Rafferty's photograph is recognised, and the Editor proclaims him to be 'Old Bill'.

1st Oct | *Birmingham Daily Mail* publishes the article "OLD BILL' Handsworth Original Of Bairnsfather Hero'. Reinforces Rafferty's claim as the original 'Old Bill'.

1918

Apr | A silent film *The Romance of Old Bill*, is released. Mr. T A Welsh is credited with taking part in the writing and producing of the film.

5th Oct	Within the pages of *John Bull* Horatio Bottomley writes: "To Capt. Bruce Bairnsfather, The Better 'Ole, France." He openly asks the question: "...don't you think you ought to make arrangements...to give her [Kate Rafferty] a handsome pension?"
Nov-Dec	Communications by letter between Mr. I Smith of Uneeda Film Service and Kate Rafferty about making a film about the life of Thomas Henry Rafferty, her husband, as the inspiration for 'Old Bill'. Kate hands over her husband's diaries to Uneeda Film Service.
13th/16th/20th Dec	Advertisements in the *Manchester Evening News* and *Manchester Evening Chronicle* advertising "Bairnsfather's Immortal play *The Better 'Ole* with a personal appearance of Mrs. Kate Rafferty as the wife of the late Old Bill."
20th Dec	As the widow of 'Old Bill', Kate appears on stage at the Manchester Palladium, apparently through her connection with Uneeda films, according to a letter within the archive. She receives a payment and a Commemorative Peace medal. (The proprietor of the Palladium was a Mr. Smith, but I could find no connection with Mr. I Smith of Uneeda Film Service.)

1919

18th Jan	Kate receives a letter from Mr. I Smith informing her that he will be travelling to America for a short while. This is the last Kate will hear from Uneeda Film Service.
Apr-Sep	Kate Rafferty receives letters from the editor of the Periodical *John Bull* (Horatio Bottomley). It is evident that she requested him to investigate the whereabouts of Mr. I Smith of Uneeda Films and her husband's diaries. Unfortunately, he has no success.
28th Aug	Kate receives a second War Gratuity payment of £5.

1922	The Cenotaph Memorial, Birmingham to the transport workers. Thomas Rafferty appears as one of those listed. (Ill:20).
1923	Memorial plaque installed on the left of the rear wall at St Peter's Church, Grove Lane, Handsworth, Birmingham. Dedicated by the Archdeacon and unveiled by Captain Newton Walsh.
1928	Kate Rafferty employed a private detective, G M McDonald, to locate soldiers who served with her husband Thomas Rafferty, without success.

1936

| July | Ivy Rafferty (27) marries Charlie Roger Dobbins (28). Ivy is recorded as working on masonic clothing, whilst Charlie works as a doctor's chauffeur. |

1953

| 16th Feb | Kate Rafferty dies aged 72. |

1959

29th Sep	Bruce Bairnsfather dies aged 72 having never publicly acknowledged that he knew Thomas Rafferty.
1990	Ivy Rafferty, now 78, passes on her mother's archive concerning Thomas Rafferty, and I begin my research.
22nd May	After reading some of my research the biographers of Bruce Bairnsfather agree that Thomas Rafferty has the best claim to be the original 'Old Bill'. Upon reading the evidence, other historians take a similar view.
1992	*The Independent* "Old Bill Identified after 77 years in that 'Ole" by Will Bennet.

	The Bygone Birmingham 'More Old Bill'. Articles in the *Western Front Association* and *The Antelope* the journal of the Royal Warwickshire Regiment.
1994	I visit Mr. Cyril Rollins, the son of Mr. S Rollins who served alongside Thomas Rafferty in peace time and the First World War. He gave me information and a picture of the Royal Warwickshire Regimental Band showing his father, uncle, and Thomas Rafferty, (Ill.2).
2000	
1st May	Ivy Rafferty dies aged 82.
2014	
Aug	I travel to The Menin Gate in Belgium to honour my great uncle, Thomas Henry Rafferty.
2015	I discover Bairnsfather's article 'Have I Insulted the British Army', and Horatio Bottomley's letter in *John Bull* at the British Library news desk. Both items add greatly to the story of Thomas Rafferty and provide, arguably, conclusive evidence that he is indeed the original 'Old Bill'.
22nd Nov	*The Sunday Times* publish the article, 'Old on, That's Uncle Tom in that 'Ole' that discusses my recent discovery of the Bairnsfather article in the context of my research.

The following chapters are, on the whole, transcriptions of correspondence or newspaper articles from the years 1914-1923. Of these, the overwhelming majority, are from Kate Rafferty's own personal archive of material, and passed on to me by her daughter, Ivy Rafferty, in 1990. The most notable exception is the article I found in the British Library written by Captain Bruce Bairnsfather, 'Have I Insulted the British Army?', and discussed extensively within Part I of this book. All the photographs of Thomas Rafferty also came from Kate Rafferty's archive, aside from the image given to me by C Rollins of the Royal Warwickshire band showing his father, uncle and Rafferty.

Part II

The Documentary Evidence

The 'Plugstreet Wood' photograph, believed to have been taken by Bairnsfather. Note the similarity between Thomas Rafferty, (far right), and Bairnsfather's cartoon character 'Old Bill'.

Lt. Bruce Bairnsfather, in the Plugstreet Wood area, 1914. Photo from Duncan Bairnsfather's photo album.

3

Message in a Bottle

MESSAGE IN A BOTTLE.

BIRMINGHAM MEN "OFF TO THE FINAL AT BERLIN."

A novel method of communicating with one's friends has just come to light. The Postmaster-General has just forwarded to Mrs. Rafferty, 8, Halliley Street, Handsworth, a message which was enclosed in a bottle picked up at Brightstone, Isle of Wight, on the 5th of November. It appears to have been thrown into the sea from a ship conveying men belonging to the Royal Warwickshire Regiment. The communication reads as follows: "Sunday, September 20th.—From some boys of the Warwicks off for the final at Berlin. Signed, T. H. Rafferty, J. H. Scott, S. Rollins, S. W. Owen, T. C. L. Rosser, T. Hubball, and B. Rawlins." The first three, at least, are Birmingham tramway employees. On the other side of the paper was the further message: "All the boys merry under strenuous conditions. Hope the finder is O.K. Write to wife and baby."

The Birmingham Daily Mail 21st November 1914

Message in a Bottle: Birmingham Men "Off To The Final At Berlin"

A novel method of communicating with one's friends has just come to light. The Postmaster-General has just forwarded to Mrs. Rafferty, 8 Halliley [Hanley] Street, Handsworth, a message that was enclosed in a bottle, picked up at Brightstone, Isle of Wight on the 5th of November. It appears to have been thrown into the sea from a ship conveying men belonging to the Royal Warwickshire Regiment. The communication reads as follows: "Sunday, September 20th. From some boys of the Warwicks off for the final at Berlin. Signed, T. H. Rafferty, J. H. Scott, S. Rollins, S. W. Owen, T. C. L. Rosser, T. Hubball and B. Rawlins." The first three, at least, are Birmingham tramway employees. On the other side of the paper was the further message: "All the boys merry under strenuous conditions. Hope the finder is O.K. Write to wife and baby."

4

The Picture Post

The Picture Post Friday 16th April 1915

Happy Group of Warwick's in a "Rabbit Hole" in the Trenches

Picture of a "rabbit hole" in a British trench sent by Private G. Roberts, 1st Battalion Royal Warwicks, to Miss G. Turner, Heneage Street, Birmingham.

Left to right: "Little Babe" Roberts; "Darkey" Revill, "the coke* carrier"; Lapham, "the fire-lighter"; Biddulph, "the stoker"; Rawlins, "the chef"; and Tom Rafferty, "the Black Hand Commander." (*Coke is produced by heating coal at high temperatures.)

5

The Bairnsfather Letter (handwritten)

FROM
CAPT. BRUCE BAIRNSFATHER,
BISHOPTON
STRATFORD-ON-AVON.
OR, c/o "BYSTANDER"
TALLIS STREET, LONDON, E.C.

August 30th

Mrs Rafferty

I am sorry I could not send back the photos of your husband sooner, but Captain Bairnsfather was away when they first came and so I kept them for him to see on his return last night. Captain Bairnsfather says he thinks it is the same photograph as the one he took, but he is very sorry indeed that he can not tell you anything about your husband as he never saw or heard anything of the men after, and only saw them once at the time he took the photograph. He is very sorry indeed

(Above and over the page) Bairnsfather's letter in which he denies that Thomas Rafferty is the inspiration for 'Old Bill'. Written by Edward Kelly, Bairnsfather's secretary.

to hear of your trouble and would
have been only too glad to tell you
any thing about your husband if he
could have done.

Captain Bairnsfather wishes me to tell
you it was the second and not the
first man from the camera that
he called "Old Bill" so from your
letter that is not your husband
as you say he was the first man
near the camera. I return all
three photographs & regret very
much that Captain Bairnsfather
is unable to give you any news
about your husband.

Yours truly,
Edward Kelly (Secretary)

5. The Bairnsfather Letter

From   August 30th [1915]

CAPT BRUCE BAIRNSFATHER

BISHOPTON   Mrs Rafferty

STRATFORD-ON-AVON

Or c/o "BYSTANDER"

Tallis Street London, E C

I am sorry I could not send back the photos of your husband sooner but Captain Bairnsfather was away when they first came and so I kept them for him to see on his return last night, Captain Bairnsfather says he thinks it is the same photograph as the one he took but he is very sorry indeed that he cannot tell you anything about your husband as he never saw or heard anything of the men after, and only saw them there once at the time he took the photograph. He is very sorry indeed to hear of your trouble and would have been only too glad to tell you anything about your husband if he could have done.

Captain Bairnsfather wished me to tell you it was the second and not the first man from the camera that he called "OLD BILL" so from your letter that is not your husband as you say he was the first man near the camera. I return all three photographs. I regret very much that Captain Bairnsfather is unable to give you any news about your husband.

Yours Truly,

Edward Kelly (secretary)

6

Bairnsfather's Alleged 'Insult' to the British Army

The Times Literary Supplement, 21st December 1916

The Soldier Who Made The Empire Laugh

It is always disappointing to be dull when others hold their sides, to be the only one, when one does not see the joke. We regret unfeigned that while the Empire laughs we must remain Dumb.

Captain Bairnsfather's cartoons have always been looked for with eagerness by the public for many months past by civilians and soldiers alike who all unite in a chorus of praise that "It is like what trench life must be". That it shows a unique British sense of humour and so on. Mr. R Kipling one may say created "The British Soldier" in the shade of Private S Ortheris and Soldiers Three what is the public reaction on reading these works, they think no soldier a "Real Soldier" unless he has plenty of the worst language, young soldiers model themselves on Private Ortheris with what results they may acquire his vices and outlook. Readers of Mr. Wells last book will remember the cockney soldier of the new army who could not open his mouth without using the word "Bloody" not that he liked it but he became Ortheris, his ideal soldier, did so and the disgust that he unleashed on his fellow soldiers when preferred = Shall we say Wordworth's Ideal; takes as his type we know of a Battalion where a soldier such as Captain Bairnsfather's takes as his type would be most summarily dealt with. Nothing so quickly lowers moral as slovenliness and nothing more difficult to check than the gradual degeneration due to trench life; and yet we have an army officer who invariably depicts his men to whom his book is dedicated use the very type which the army is anxious to suppress, can it be wondered at the young soldiers try to look like a "Bairnsfather type".

We can all remember the Gibson Girl but do we want our daughters to look like "Eve" is another of our illustrated contemporaries: yet "Eve" is delightful because she is not degenerative she is impossible.

Bairnsfather's Alf and Bert are disgusting because they are possible, it is not with Captain Bairnsfather's humour that we quarrel for his are invariably amusing it is because he standardises almost idealises a degraded type of face. We cannot but enter a protest against a cruel caricature of the men who endured the first winter in France. The men we knew joked and swore like many other gallant men, out there they prided themselves as being the smartest Battalion in the Brigade. Not the one that resembles one of Bairnsfather's drawings, as to the two books before us *Bullets and Billets* (Grant Richards 5s net) – and *Bairnsfather – Fragments from his Life* (Hodder and Stoughton 3s and 6 pence net) – The former is a little book of sketches of a type which we are all familiar they are well enough done to be a pleasure to read but most interest lies in the pictures. The latter is a most elaborate life of the artist by a friend, a life not so remarkable and varied as to deserve such a reward – if we may call it so.

Kipling's Three Soldiers – Learoyde, Mulvaney and Stanley Ortheris are from Kipling's stories of soldiers in Afghanistan in the nineteenth century.

The Gibson Girl appeared in illustrations by Charles Dana Gibson in the 1890s where the artist sought to present an image of the All American Girl.

7

Bairnsfather's Riposte

The Weekly Dispatch London, 5th August 1917

"Have I Insulted The British Army?"

By Capt Bruce Bairnsfather, in an interview.

Nothing so quickly lowers 'moral' as slovenliness and nothing more difficult to check than the gradual degeneration due to trench life, and yet we have an Army officer who invariably depicts his men (to whom his book is dedicated) as the very type which the Army is anxious to suppress. Can it be wondered at that young soldiers try to look like a "Bairnsfather type"? We can all remember the "Gibson Girl" but do we want our daughters to look like "Eve" in another of our illustrated contemporaries? Yet "Eve" is delightful because she is not a degenerate she is an impossible. Bairnsfather's Alf and Bert are disgusting because they are so possible. It is not with Captain Bairnsfather's humour that we quarrel, for his situations are invariably amusing. It is because he standardises – almost idealises – a degraded type of face. We cannot but enter a protest against so cruel a caricature of the men who endured the first winter in France – The Times Literary Supplement in a review of Captain Bairnsfather's sketches. [TLS dated 21st December 1916]

Old Bill, Bert and Alf are not creations of an artist's fanciful brain. They lived and had their being (they were mostly Cockneys and Wolverhampton and Birmingham men) in a watery slit in the ground, somewhere in the Ypres Salient, in the never-to-be-forgotten days of the first year of the war. I knew them well because I lived and fought with them. I listened daily to their jokes, and shared their joys and sorrows. They were not degraded or disgusting.

They used powerful and full-flavoured English 'tis true, but they used it, more often than not, as part of their ever-buoyant outlook on life. They saw humour while up to their waists in icy-cold water: they poked unceasing fun at everything and everybody – especially at Fritz. The more severe the hardships, the more developed was their humour. Their vices were far and away outnumbered by their virtues.

"Old Bill" was as gentle a fighting man as ever shouldered a rifle. He couldn't possibly be dressed smartly under the conditions under which he existed. He had been a very smart soldier before he was taken away from an Aldershot barrack room to make one of a draft of French's "Contemptible little Army".

When we remember what he went through – the bitter hardships he bore, the make-shifts he put up with, the prodigies of valour he performed at Mons and Ypres and elsewhere – is it any wonder that he cultivated a walrus-moustache and wore a disreputable-looking Balaclava "woolley" over a tattered khaki tunic?

I have invented nothing. This photograph I took in Plug-street Wood in 1914, and here you see for the first time the originals of Old Bill, Bert, and Alf as I knew them and portrayed them.

Alf   Bert   Old Bill

People who say I libelled the British Army do not know the Old Army that sent the First Expeditionary Force to France. Without in the least disparaging the fighting qualities of the New Army, it is quite obvious to anyone who knows the constitution and temperament of both the Old and the New, that the Mons men were of a type quite different from the men who are fighting so worthily today. It was in the Mons army that Old Bill and his two pals were to be found almost exclusively.

Now in an army of all ranks of civilian life, they are becoming more and more difficult to find. Presently you will be able to get a big price for a real "Old Bill" in the flesh.

The old type has largely given place to a new type of soldier. The new man is just as good a fighter and just as good a comrade, but he has a different outlook and temperament from his predecessor of the old days.

Comparatively speaking, those days are over; our Army has all it wants and more than it wants. Old Bill and his pals, Bert and Alf have "gone west", most of them. Those of his type who have come safely through are either at home instructing the soldier of to-day or invalided out of the service.

Now and again you meet an "Old Bill" in France – my brother wrote recently saying he had found one in his company. I get hundreds of letters from the front saying "Old Bill says so-and-so" or "Bert he up and says so-and-so." All the writers use the characters, I have focused upon and made popular with the Army.

I have invented nothing; and all that knew the men of the Old Army know that Old Bill, Bert and Alf were but types of a wonderful company, the like of which will, in all probability, never be seen again.

My three Characters were not in a War, They were at War.

8

'Old Bill' Identified

HOW WAR TRANSFORMS
THE MAN.

"Old Bill," when he was plain Thomas Rafferty before the war.

"Old Bill," as he was photographed in the trenches by Captain Bairnsfather.

The Weekly Dispatch London 30th September 1917

"The Weekly Dispatch" Discovers The Original of "Old Bill"
Bairnsfather's Great War Character was Once a tramway worker in Birmingham.

Old Bill belonged to Birmingham. Bairnsfather's immortal creation once worked on a tramway-car in the Midland capital.

There is no doubt about his identity. Officials and mates vouch that Old Bill was one of their company, and his wife is similarly satisfied. Besides the Editor of *The Weekly Dispatch* has received photographic evidence that the man Bairnsfather knew and the man that Bairnsfather created have one and the same personality. In Bairnsfather's delightful and intimate portraiture of the Gapper Tommy they recognise Old Bill, who on duty and off in Birmingham was the same unmistakable individual, cheery, humorous, commanding, picturesque, and, above all, a man's man, able to inspire at once respect and affection, a pal and a foreman.

Mention Pat Rafferty to the Birmingham tramway men on the Handsworth route, and a broad smile, such as Old Bill loved, envelope their features. "Ah! You mean Old Bill," they say.

Rafferty was a soldier who loved soldiering for soldiering's sake. He had served his time in the Royal Warwicks and been transferred to the Reserve when, in the middle of 1909, he joined the Birmingham Corporation Tramways, and thence onwards until 1913 served as motor-man, when he became acting inspector, promoted for merit. At the outbreak of war, on leaving to join his regiment in the Isle of Wight he stood at the back of a tram-way car going from Handsworth to the city and breezily called out to his mates who were wishing him "Good luck and a safe return": "So long boys, we'll soon have this job over, and then I'll be with you again."

Alas! Rafferty, for all his qualities, was neither a prophet nor the son of a prophet; the job was not destined to be over soon, and he was not destined to return. He lies, poor fellow, somewhere in France or Flanders, with two years' soil over his head – so much they know in Birmingham – but he did his duty and played the game as those who have him in tender recollection knew he would, and in the Valhalla of humble patriots he has a place and a niche, than which even the greatest among us can wish for no finer reward.

They didn't call him Old Bill in Birmingham before the war. They called him "Pat."

When you are known to your mates as a racial sobriquet you have earned their affection.

Among his class Rafferty led. In an argument his was the opinion that prevailed. You might be cleverer and more pungent, but Rafferty's say held the field.

"If Pat says it is so, then it is so." That clinched it. Immaterial whether Rafferty was right or wrong, he had his way. In that sense he was a great man in a little world. He was honoured in his own country, of scant screage though it may have been. The proof of this also is easy to seek.

Old Bill had that rare gift we describe as "Initiative." He didn't wait on his fellows; they waited on him. When there was a tramway block it was Old Bill to whom they looked to put things right.

Old Bill, instinctively assumed the part, rarely disappointed them. Imagine a score of cars held up in a line and Rafferty the driver of the rearmost; it would be a sorry moment for general expectation if he didn't step off his car, push himself to the front, apply himself to the mischief, and get things right.

All of us in our own walks of life must have met the type, for Old Bill was not so much a distinct generation as a type – men in the bulk are more or less sheep waiting to be led; and Rafferty was one of those who led. Born to greater things, he must have achieved greatness, since the essence of greatness, leadership, was in him, and leadership, as the truthful will admit, is not a matter of red tabs; it is personality.

Soldier habits persist, and they recall of Rafferty that his buttons were always well polished and that there was an almost fastidious neatness about his get up. He had the old soldier's naïve faith in the prowess of British arms and didn't believe that any other nation could produce soldiers to touch ours. He smiled at the idea of the Germans, "miserable, under-fed blighters," as he conceived them, standing up to a regiment of British Regulars.

Old Bill doted on being in the picture. Call it weakness or what you will, but unless you grant that sense of personal pride to him your image is faulty. He liked music and was a member of the Tram-way Band. His instrument was the big drum, no doubt chosen because it made the most noise and set our hero apart from the rest. How he thumped that drum – the Homeric energy of the man – the genial, agreeable concert of his performance – these are reflections that in no way diminish his stature but round off the pleasant shadow it cast.

At the depot it was Rafferty's merry voice: "Well, now, whose call is it?" which inevitably prefaced a spell of conviviality, for even in these things he led the way. He was a temperate man, while never at a difficulty to accommodate himself to his company. He "stood his corner" without throwing his money about; he was never short without being flush; he could always be relied upon for a bit on account without suggesting that he made a habit of it. A very well-balanced, picturesque figure of a man was Old Bill.

It was characteristic of Old Bill that when leaving the Isle of Wight for France he should have wished to send a message to his pals in Birmingham, and it was equally characteristic of Old Bill to choose as a means of communication a sealed bottle thrown into the sea, which bottle with its hasty scrawl in due course turned up at Birmingham. "He always had plenty of 'savvy," is the comment of his mates on this incident. "Trust Old Bill to get round a difficulty."

As for the rest, it need only be said that the identification of Rafferty as Old Bill came through the publication of the photograph of Bairnsfather's hero in The Weekly Dispatch. His friends saw it and immediately exclaimed: "That's Pat Rafferty." This was a month ago. Birmingham, which had a right to claim a wonderful character in the British Army, for three years never knew it. How often is this the way of greatness!

9

'Old Bill' Newspaper Article

Birmingham Daily Mail 1st October 1917

"OLD BILL" Handsworth Original Of Bairnsfather Hero.

The "Weekly Dispatch" (London) claims to have established by means of a photograph the identity of the original of Captain Bairnsfather's "Old Bill," the hero of so many of his best cartoons and the exemplification of the cheery spirit of the old British Army. "Old Bill," who is said to have been photographed by Captain Bairnsfather in the trenches, was Acting-Tramway Inspector Patrick Rafferty, of the Birmingham Tramway Department, stationed on the Handsworth route.

Rafferty was a soldier who loved soldiering for soldiering's sake. He had served his time in the Royal Warwicks and been transferred to the Reserve when, in the middle of 1909, he joined the Birmingham Corporation Tramways, and thence onwards until 1913 served as motor-man, when he became acting inspector, promoted for merit. At the outbreak of war, on leaving to join his regiment in the Isle of Wight, he stood at the back of a tramway-car going from Handsworth to the city and breezily called out to his mates who were wishing him 'Good luck and a safe return.' 'So long boys; we'll soon have this job over, and then I'll be with you again.' Alas! Rafferty, for all his qualities, was neither a prophet nor the son of a prophet; the job was not destined to be over soon, and he was not destined to return. He lies, poor fellow, somewhere in France or Flanders, with two years' soil over his head – so much they know in Birmingham – but he did his duty and played the game as those who have him in tender recollection knew he would, and in the Valhalla of humble patriots he has a place and a niche, than which even the greatest among us can wish for no finer reward.

Soldier habits persist, and they recall of Rafferty that his buttons were always well polished and that there was an almost fastidious neatness about his get-up. He had the old soldier's naïve faith in the prowess of British arms and didn't believe that any other nation could produce soldiers to touch ours.

He smiled at the idea of the Germans, 'miserable, under-fed blighters,' as he conceived them, standing up to a regiment of British Regulars. Old Bill doted on being in the picture. He liked music and was a member of the Tramway Band. His instrument was the big drum, no doubt chosen because it made the most noise and set our hero apart from the rest. How he thumped that drum – the Homeric energy of the man – the genial, agreeable concert of this performance – these are reflections that in no ways diminish his stature but round off the pleasant shadow it cast.

It was characteristic of Old Bill that when leaving the Isle of Wight for France he should have wished to send a message to his pals in Birmingham, and it was equally characteristic of Old Bill to choose as a means of communication a sealed bottle thrown into the sea, which bottle with its hasty scrawl in due course turned up at Birmingham. 'He always had plenty of savvy,' is the comment of his mates on this incident. 'Trust Old Bill to get round a difficulty.'

10

Horatio Bottomley's Intervention

October 5th, 1918

John Bull weekly magazine

Editor Mr. Horatio Bottomley

Candid Communications,

TO CAPT BRUCE BAIRNSFATHER, THE BETTER 'OLE, FRANCE

DEAR CAP, – That there is a Better 'Ole – some-where about I know from the pictures, but for some reason or other the widow of old Bill doesn't seem to be in it. Rafferty was his name in the flesh – Pat Rafferty, the Birmingham tramways inspector. He was a soldier long before you, an artist, dug in with him. Though you have turned him dead and alive into a pictorial fortune, and play-producers and actor-managers and film-makers have made thousands of pounds out of his beloved memory, not one of the crowd seems even to have given a thought or cared a damn for the poor struggling widow and the child left behind. Say a slight token of gratitude to Old Bill don't you think you ought to make arrangements among you to give her a handsome pension?

John Bull

11

Film Contract and Correspondence
with Uneeda Film Service

First letter from Uneeda Film Service dated 21st November 1918 (typed):

Mrs. Rafferty, 57 Baker Street, Handsworth, Birmingham.

Dear Madam

I have been in communication with Mr. Bottomley for some time in connection with a paragraph he had in his paper with reference to yourself and the film – "THE BETTER 'OLE", with the idea of seeing what could be done whereby you would derive some benefit from the film in which your late husband was featured. I have several suggestions at issue, but should like to see you to make some definite arrangements. I should therefore be obliged if you would arrange to come to Manchester on Monday and I herewith enclose telegram, which you can use to wire me if you can get up. There is a good train leaves New Street at 9-10 arrives here at 11-47 on Monday morning. Please wire me.

Yours Faithfully,
I. Smith

Second letter from Uneeda Film Service dated 25th November 1918 (long hand):

Mrs. Rafferty, 57 Baker Street, Bham.

Dear Madam,

The Writer not having heard from you yesterday before leaving the office is taking the liberty of enclosing £1 in the event of your being able to come through to Manchester tomorrow Monday.

In the event of your not being able to catch the 9-10 train then there is another at 10-45 and another 11-38 if you have not wired which train you will come by I shall be glad if you will do so.

Yours Faithfully,
I. Smith

Third letter: a contract with Uneeda Film Contract dated 25th November 1918 (typed):

I Mrs. Kate Rafferty, Wife of the late "Old Bill" of 57 Baker Street, Handsworth, Birmingham, A G R E E –

With MESSRS THE UNEEDA FILM SERVICE of the above address (or their Assignees) to place my services in their hands exclusively, for the purposes of producing a film, in which I personally am to appear relating to the life of my late husband.

THE UNEEDA FILM SERVICE agree to pay me 10% on the net proceeds of the profit of the said film, with a minimum of £100 and they further agree to pay me all out of pocket expenses.

Signed by Kate Rafferty
I. Smith, 64 Victoria St, Manchester

Fourth letter from Uneeda Film Service dated 25th November 1918:

Mrs. Rafferty, 57 Baker Street, Bham.

Dear Madam,

I herewith enclose copy of Agreement you have signed today. I further Enclose a rough copy of a few details I specially require. I feel sure you will get all the information together you can by tomorrow night, and despatch it to me.

Kind Regards,
Yours Faithfully
I. Smith

Fifth letter Uneeda Film Service dated 27th November 1918 (typed):

Dear Madam,

I received the four books this morning quite safely, for which many thanks, I have not had a letter from you but anticipate it being in the post. If you have not already given in your letter the following details, I should be glad if you would do so.

Whom your Husband's parents were?
Where your Husband was born?
School attended
Worked when married
Wife's Occupation before marriage
Where met
When he joined the Army
What leave and when
Have you any letters from him
Has he told you of any of his life experiences
What age

Yours Faithfully
I. Smith

Sixth letter Uneeda Film Service dated 2nd December 1918 (typed):

Mrs. Rafferty, 57 Baker Street, BIRMINGHAM

Dear Mrs. Rafferty,

I have your kind letter also enclosures, for which I thank you. I hope to be leaving for London tomorrow, and get the business in hand, we shall doubtless have some news for you shortly.

Yours Faithfully
I. Smith

Seventh letter Uneeda Film Service 13th December 1918 (typed):

Mrs. Rafferty, Baker Street, Handsworth, BIRMINGHAM

Dear Mrs. Rafferty,

We are getting things nicely in hand and hope to make a start on the film immediately after Christmas. Regarding next week at the Palladium Manchester would you arrange to call at our office at 54 Victoria Street (these if you remember are the second offices you come to), at any time between five and six thirty as we should like your presence on Friday evening at the Palladium when we hope to present you with a substantial amount. If you require any expenses let us know and we will send them on.

Yours Faithfully
I. Smith

Eighth letter Uneeda Film Service 18th January 1919 (long hand):

Telephone   Telegraphic Address: "Famfilm." Manchester

Uneeda Film Service

Proprietor, I. Smith

Official Agents For   49 Deansgate

Topical Budget   Manchester Jan 18th 1919

Under the supervision of
the Ministry of Information

Dear Mrs. Rafferty,

I am afraid you will think things are progressing rather slow, but I have been very busy, and I am leaving for America in a few days, but for the short time I am away I am leaving everything in one of my partner's hands.

His address is Mr. W Millward, The Cinema Club, Ormes Bdgs, The Parsonage, Manchester.

I hope you arrived home safe and sound.

Kindest Regards,
Yours Sincerely
Mr. I. Smith

12

Adverts for Manchester Palladium Theatre Play

THE PALLADIUM,
Peter-street.
"MY UNMARRIED WIFE;"
A High-Class Domestic Play, and
SPECIAL ATTRACTIONS.
Continuous Performance 1 to 5, & 6-50 to 10-50 p.m.

PALLADIUM. TO-NIGHT.
Mrs. RAFFERTY, wife of the late T. Rafferty
(Old Bill), will be presented by the Management
with a PURSE OF TREASURY NOTES, which has
been subscribed by the Management and Audiences
this week, when showing the film featuring her
husband, "THE BETTER 'OLE."

Newspaper advertisement referencing Kate Rafferty's planned appearance at the play 'The Better 'Ole'.

PALLADIUM, Peter Street – *Manchester Evening Chronicle,* 13th Dec 1918

Next Week Mon, Tues, & Wed, Bairnsfather's Immortal Play "The Better 'Ole" Thurs, Fri, & Sat "My Unmarried Wife". Friday Night a personal appearance of Mrs. Rafferty, Wife of Late "Old Bill"

PALLADIUM Peter Street, Next Week – *Manchester Evening News,* 13th Dec 1918

MONDAY TUESDAY and WEDNESDAY Bairnsfather's Immortal Play-- "THE BETTER 'OLE" Thursday; Fri Personal Appearance of Mrs. Rafferty, wife of the late OLD BILL

THE PALLADIUM, Peter Street – *Manchester Evening News,* 16th Dec 1918

Bairnsfather's Immortal Play – THE BETTER 'OLE and tasteful Comedy and interesting Program, Part of the proceeds are being handed to the wife of the Late "OLD BILL". Prices and Times as usual

PALLADIUM TONIGHT – *Manchester Evening Chronicle,* 20th Dec 1918

Mrs. Rafferty, wife of the late T Rafferty "OLD BILL" will be presented by the Management with a Purse of Treasury Notes, which has been subscribed by the Management and the Audience this week when showing the Film featuring her late Husband "THE BETTER 'OLE"

13

Horatio Bottomley Investigates

First letter to Kate Rafferty:

ID/D

JOHN BULL   Editorial Offices

Telephone Gerrard 9637 or 9638   93 Long Acre

Telegraphic Address   London WC2

"Heroically London"   April 7th 1919

Dear Madam, I regret that, owing to great pressure of business, I have not acknowledged your letter. I am sorry to hear of your complaint and if you will send me any correspondence you have had with Mr. Smith, I will try to get in touch with him and enquire into the matter. I enclose special envelope for your reply.

Yours Faithfully,
The Editor.

Second letter to Kate Rafferty:

ID/D

JOHN BULL   Editorial Offices

Telephone Gerrard 9637 or 9638   93 Long Acre

Telegraphic Address   London WC2

"Heroically London"   May 1st 1919

Mrs. K Rafferty, 57 Baker Street, Handsworth, Birmingham.

Dear Madam, with reference to your letter, I have endeavoured to get in touch with Mr. Smith of the "Uneeda Film Service", but regret to say that my communication has been returned through the Post Office marked "Removed". Should I succeed in ascertaining his present whereabouts, I shall be only too pleased to write him again and let you know in due course the results. Meanwhile, I return the documents and photographs you were good enough to send me, With all my Wishes,

Yours Faithfully,
The Editor.

Third letter to Kate Rafferty:

ID/D

JOHN BULL	Editorial Offices
Telephone Gerrard 9637 or 9638	93 Long Acre
Telegraphic Address	London WC2
"Heroically London"	June 4th 1919

Mrs. K Rafferty, 57 Baker Street, Handsworth, Birmingham.

Dear Madam,

I duly received your letter, but, as I have already told you the difficulty is that the company seems to have left the address in Manchester and their present whereabouts are unknown. However, should I be able to trace them, I will certainly follow the matter up.

Yours Faithfully,
The Editor.

Fourth letter to Kate Rafferty:

ID/D

JOHN BULL   Editorial Offices

Telephone Gerrard 9637 or 9638   93 Long Acre

Telegraphic Address   London WC2

"Heroically London"   17th September 1919

Dear Madam,

I am sorry to say that, though I have made exhaustive enquiries, I have been unable to trace Mr. Smith or Uneeda Film Co. which seems to come to grief and disappeared. If I should get any news I will write to you at once,

With best wishes,
Yours Faithfully,
The Editor.

14

Kate Rafferty hires a Private Detective

12th Oct 1928

From, G. F. McDonald, Melrose, Grove Lane, Handsworth

Dear Mrs. Rafferty,

I have called several times at the four addresses detailed in the enclosed letters. But have always found, four houses locked, Mr. McDonald did talk to some of the people stated but the particular man you wanted could not be traced, sorry we could not do more for you.

Yours Truly
G McDonald

15

C B Rollins in the letter pages of *Bygone Birmingham* (Son of Private S Rollins, Thomas Rafferty's Companion)

More Old Bill 1992

I was very interested in the article by Karen Padjet on Old Bill in the eighth issue of *Bygone Birmingham* as I have always understood that the character was sketched from Pat Rafferty, my father [Private S Rollins] served with the 1st Battalion Royal Warwickshire Regiment from the outbreak of the First World War until the first Battle of Ypres in 1915 [clearly C B Rollins meant the Second Battle of Ypres], and he told me on more than one occasion that Bruce Bairnsfather based his sketches of Bill on Pat Rafferty, and was understood by the soldiers serving with him this was the case. Several years ago there was some discussion in the press as to the identity of "Old Bill" during which several names were put forward. But my father was surprised at this as there was no doubt whatever in his mind that it was Pat Rafferty.

C B Rollins

Part III

In Memoriam

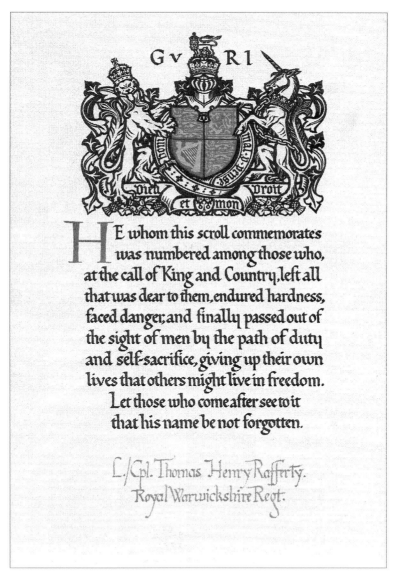

Gv R1

HE whom this scroll commemorates
was numbered among those who,
at the call of King and Country, left all
that was dear to them, endured hardness,
faced danger, and finally passed out of
the sight of men by the path of duty
and self-sacrifice, giving up their own
lives that others might live in freedom.
Let those who come after see to it
that his name be not forgotten.

L/Cpl. Thomas Henry Rafferty.
Royal Warwickshire Regt.

The Commemorative Scroll of Thomas Rafferty.

16

Royal Warwickshire Regimental Roll of WWI Casualties

List of Casualties among Officers on 25th April 1915 according to the Regimental War Diaries – Catalogue ref: WO/95/1484.

Captain H J Walker	Killed in Action
Lieutenant L Nicolan	Killed in Action
Lieutenant T O Fayne	Killed in Action
2nd Lieutenant A Jowitt	Killed in Action
2nd Lieutenant G S MacLagan	Killed in Action
2nd Lieutenant L H L Rowley	Killed in Action
2nd Lieutenant F Ricard	Killed in Action
2nd Lieutenant J Lockburn	Killed in Action
Captain T H Black	Wounded and missing
2nd Lieutenant R T Hunt	Wounded and missing
Lieutenant Lucian Smith	Missing believed killed
Captain L T Tomes	Wounded
Captain J T Britherton	Wounded
Lieutenant R B Tillyer	Wounded
2nd Lieutenant G B James	Wounded
Lieutenant A Ramsey	Wounded

Lieutenant G Care and Lieutenant B Bairnsfather to hospital suffering with shock

Soldiers who died in the First World War 25th April 1915 1st Regiment the Royal Warwickshire Regiment the same day T H Rafferty was killed in action

7050 Private Charles Henry Adams

9402 Private William Adcock

438 Private William Amey

9384 Private David Angus

9071 Private John Armfield

9887 Private Bertie Thomas Astell

2334 Private Albert Atkins

1840 Private James Bacon

6314 Private Walter Baker

4114 Private Ernest Ballard

1485 Private Alexander Barclay

9167 A/Sgt Charles Barrett

9458 Private Charles Thomas Beach

8966 Private James Arthur Beal

3342 Private Henry Bembridge

9482 L/Cpl William Eli Benson

1922 L/Sgt Arthur Bickley

2782 Private Albert Samuel Biffin

7020 Private William John Blick

1858 Private Lewis Bradshaw

4807 Private Lewis Brimble

1940 Private Peter Coyne

1614 Private Robert Craddock

6340 A/Sgt William Cranbrook

8958 Private Charles Crumpton

831 Private Joseph Leonard Daw

7631 Private William Dawson

9779 L/Cpl Harry Dennis

511 Private William Dobinson

6790 Private John Henry Doughty

2413 Private Frederick Duckerin

2393 Private Henry Eadon

9617 Private Edwin John Fane

366 Private William Finch

3274 Private C H Gartenfield

6861 Private William H Garvey

6921 Private Charles John Gear

2157 Private William H Gifford

2575 Private William P Gordon

9935 Private Benjamin G Gough

10410 Private Alfred B Govett

1204 Private W C H E Gray

1616 Private Henry Brown	1876 L/Cpl Harry Grice
1651 L/Cpl William Thomas Bullock	316 L/Cpl John Thomas Gurney
1535 Private George Henry Carter	9619 A/Cpl Frederick Hall
4260 Private John Cassel	734 Private John Hammond
2352 Private John Charlwood	2486 Private James T Hart
229 Private William George Chatland	6984 Private Frederick G Hawks
3072 Private Arthur Cherry	8995 Private James T Healey
7536 Private John William Clarke	9357 Private Alfred Heard
9222 L/Cpl Arthur Henry Cleaver	9752 Private Harry Hill
7557 Private John Clemens	400 L/Cpl John Honner
694 Private Thomas Clements	9831 Private Frederick Ingram
6324 Private Joseph Cleton	1878 Private William Ingram
7242 Private Benjamin Coates	9982 Sgt Edwin Thomas Jeynes
306 Private Frederick Coats	2117 L/Cpl Alfred Jones
8925 Private Richard Cole	2015 Private Robert Jones
9695 Private James Connor	323 A/C.Q.M.S. William Jones
2242 Private Alexander Cook	7393 Private George Kirkoff
1072 Private Albert Cort	*1448 L/Cpl Charles R Lapham
513 Private Albert Lazonby	2083 Private Frederick Oliver
9281 Private Albert Edward Lloyd	3344 Private James Osborne
571 Private John Edward Lloyd	*2824 Private George Ernest Owen
2633 Private George E Luckett	3171 Private Jasper Packer
812 L/Cpl Lenard Manchester	9159 L/Cpl Thomas Parsons

1597 Private John C Manning

9759 Private Frank Masters

2635 Private Percy W Mathews

1957 L/Cpl Alfred Maughan

6864 Private Charles McCracken

15 Private Frank Medlam

8944 Private William Middleton

9363 Private Francis W Morris

6227 L/Sgt Sidney Mulliss

50 A/Cpl Sidney J Murphy

2831 L/Cpl Walter I Newton

7498 Private Herbert Nuthall

200 Private F O'Dell

2413 Private Frederick W Duckerin

2393 Private Henry Eadon

0917 Private Edwin John Fane

366 Private William Finch

3274 Private Charles R Gartenfield

6861 Private William Hugh Garvey

6921 Private Charles John Gear

2157 Private William H Gifford

2575 Private William P Gordon

9935 Private Benjamin G Gough

10225 Private Harry Paybody

2031 L/Cpl Harry Payne

466 Private John W Pearson

2344 L/Cpl John T Perry

7193 Private Arthur Phillips

1676 Private Edwin Alfred Piper

3266 Private Arthur Charles Pitt

9346 Private James E Priest

1743 Private Albert J Probert

3255 Private George Rachel

*7840 L/Cpl Thomas H Rafferty

*7262 Private Bert Rawlins

9502 L/Cpl Thomas Robbins

*8880 Private William Roberts

9739 Private Frederick Rodds

9631 Private Frederick Russell

9853 John M Ryan

9953 Private Frank Shepherd

9395 Cpl William H Skidmore

10420 Private David Slaymaker

3264 Private Arthur Smith

7270 Private Walter Smit

1672 Private William H Smith

10410 Private Alfred B Govett

1204 Private W C H E Gray

1876 L/Cpl Harry Grice

316 L/Cpl John Thomas Gurney

9619 A/Cpl Frederick Hall

734 Private John Hammond

2486 Private James Timothy Hart

6984 Private Frederick G Hawkes

8995 Private James T Healey

9357 Private Alfred Heard

9752 Private Harry Hill

400 L/Cpl John Honner

9831 Private Frederick Ingram

1878 Private William Ingram

456 Private Sidney G Westall

429 Private Frederick Wilkinson

498 Private William Wilkshire

9525 Private Walter Soles

8804 Private Will Steadman

9187 Private Albert Steventon

9621 Sgt Norris Sturt

8970 Private William Tapp

75113 Private Joseph Taylor

763 Private Horace Tomlinson

9252 Private William Toon

3226 Private George Topping

1785 Private Richard Vallance

9851 Private Thomas Varley

9530 Private Fredrick Waldron

148 Private Charles Ward

1455 Private Samuel Ward

2260 Private George Worrel

1237 Private Arthur Wragg

9747 A/Cpl Thomas Yates

Names marked with * are mentioned in newspaper articles along with TH Rafferty's.

17

Memorial Tablet at St Peter's Parish Church

Names of those commemorated on the Memorial Tablet at St Peter's Parish Church, Grove Lane, Handsworth, Birmingham.

To members of the Royal Warwickshire and Staffordshire regiments casualties of the Great War as recorded in the Dedication of the Memorial order of service 1936.

Harry Adams, William Austin, Ernest Baker, Harry Barnsley, Archie Barton, Charles Bezer, William Bezer, Edwin Blount, Anthony Clifford, Frank Ernest Cook, John Coman, Henry Darby, Horace Darby, George Dewsbury, Harold Doughty, Sidney William Fisher, Herbert Foly, William Henry Fripp, Philip Gilbert, Arthur Gocher, Alfred Goode, Walter Harry Grant, John William Hancock, Bailey Harker, Philip Harrison, Charles Healey, Albert Edward Hemming, John Heyland, Edward Lake, Herbert Latimer, Thomas Edward Long, John Manison, Arthur Mears, Sidney Mears, Neville Loyde Parton, Ronald Piper, Horace Quiney, Thomas Henry Rafferty, Reece Richardson, George Smelt, Thomas Snape, Leonard Birkett Taylor, Frank Edwin Thorn, William Fredrick Thorn, Harold Thorpe, Ernest Trueman, Herbert Wakelin, Richard Williams, Gordon White, Arthur Whiting, Thomas Whiting and C Whitley.

Forty-seven thousand five hundred men enlisted in the thirteen Battalions of the Royal Warwickshire Regiments that fought in all theatres of the Great War. The regimental roll contains the names of eleven thousand four hundred and forty-five men who gave their lives during the four year conflict. There were many awards for bravery including six Victoria Crosses awarded to soldiers of the Royal Warwickshire Regiment.

Bibliography

Allen C, *Soldier Sahibs: The Men Who Made the North-West Frontier* (2012 Hachette) p.104 discusses Uniform Colours.

Bailey B, 'Cartoonist at War' *This England* (c.1996 D C Thompson).

Bairnsfather B, *Bullets and Billets* (1917 Grant Richards).

Bairnsfather B, 'Have I Insulted The British Army?' *The Weekly Dispatch London* (5/8/1917).

Bairnsfather B, 'Old Bill and I: You Never Know, Do You?' *Birmingham Weekly Post & Midland Pictorial* (02/01/1959).

Bairnsfather B, 'Old Bill and I: Slithering About in Plugstreet Wood.' *Birmingham Weekly Post & Midland Pictorial* (09/01/1959).

Bairnsfather B, 'Old Bill and I: Walking in the Mud Like Chimpanzees.' *Birmingham Weekly Post & Midland Pictorial* (16/01/1959).

Baker C, Birmingham History Forum (Memorials).

Belcher J, 'Birmingham's Old Bill: Thomas Henry Rafferty' *Carl Chinn's Brummagem*. Issue 176 (November 2015).

Bennet W, 'Old Bill Identified After 77 Years In That 'Ole' *The Independent* (26th May 1992).

Birmingham Library (Wolfson Centre ref no EP/7/4 St Peter's WWI Memorial tablet).

British Film Institute. Films on 'Old Bill'.

British Library, London, news desk.

Buxton G, *Time to Remember, Journal of Lance Sergeant William Web* (2016 Exeter: Helion & Company) p.83 discusses the engagement at Meteren, Belgium.

Census and National Archives (Kew National Army Museum, effects and ledgers WWI ref no-247118).

'Creator of "Old Bill" dies' *Birmingham Weekly Post & Midland Pictorial* (02/10/1959).

Duckers P, *North West Frontier 1908: The Zakka Khel & Mohmand Campaigns* (2006 Spink & Son Ltd) p.90 references W Biddulph.

Haldane A, *A Brigade of the Old Army, 1914* (2015 Naval & Military Press).

Dr Hanna E, 'Myth and Reality, the Christmas Truce 1914' *Western Front Association* Bulletin (March 2015).

Hart C J, *The Royal Warwickshire Regiment* (1906 The Midlands Counties Herald limited).

'Happy Group of Warwick's in a Rabbit Hole' *Picture Post* (16/04/1915).

Hellen N and Gillespie J. 'Old on, That's Uncle Tom in that 'Ole'. *The Times* (22/11/2015).

Holt T & V, *In Search of the Better 'Ole: A Biography of Captain Bruce Bairnsfather* (2001 Pen & Sword).

Hutton J, *August 1914 Surrender at St Quentin* (2010 Pen & Sword).

Kingsford C L, *The Warwickshire Regiment* (First edition c.1920 Country Life, reprinted in 1997 by D P & G Military Publishers Doncaster).

Manchester Library (play advertisements).

'Message in a Bottle' *The Birmingham Daily Mail* (21/11/1914).

Ministry of Defence. Bourne Ave, Hayes Middlesex, England UB3 1RF.

'More Old Bill' Letters Page *Bygone Birmingham* (1992).

Naval and Military Press *Soldiers Died in the Great War 1914-19: A Complete and Searchable Digital Database.* (2004 CD-rom).

'OLD BILL.' Handsworth Original of Bairnsfather Hero *The Birmingham Daily Mail* (01/10/1917).

Reed A, *Meet at Dawn Unarmed: Captain Robert Hamilton's Account of Trench Warfare and the Christmas Truce in 1914* (2009 Dene House Publishing).

This England Summer 1991, 'English County Regiments', (p.56).

Sheffield Archives (Sheffield Equalised Independent Druids).

Smith D H MBE, *From Trams to Trenches: the story of Birmingham Corporation Tramways workers who gave their lives in the First World War* (2014 National Express).

Shephard B, *A War of Nerves: Soldiers and Psychiatrists 1914-1994* (2000 London Jonathan Cape).

Terraine J, *The Great War 1914/18* (1965 Hutchinson & Co Ltd) pp.137/138 gives an account of the Second Battle of Ypres.

'The Soldier Who Made The Empire Laugh' *The Times Literary Supplement* (21/12/1916).

'The Weekly Dispatch Discovers The Original of "Old Bill"' *The Weekly Dispatch London* (30/09/1917).

The author at The Menin Gate, August 2014.

John Belcher was born on 13th October 1948 in Washwood Heath, Birmingham. He was educated at Ward End Hall Secondary School and left at the tender age of 15 with no qualifications to become a carpenter. He married a local girl Maxine Dorothy Allen and with a passion for all things wood he became an Associate of the British Institute of Certified Carpenters. Later in life he decided to take up War Studies at Birmingham University and also became a Magistrate at Solihull Courts. Now retired after a lifetime as a carpenter he continues to have a passion for military history.

Thomas Small has a life-long fascination with history, studying archaeology at the University of Newcastle-Upon-Tyne, and going on to work for various archaeological organisations throughout the UK. He now lives in East Lothian and works as a freelance illustrator drawing everything from archaeological artefacts to graphics panels for local museums. When not illustrating, he can be found beachcombing the local coastline, and immersing himself in the history of the area. Examples of his work can be viewed at www.smallfindsdesign.co.uk.